Inner Cheerleader

To, Samantha,

The Greatest Cheerleader
I have ever met.

18/7/2012.

Happy Birthday
Love Chris x.

Your
Inner Cheerleader

A Guide to Master
The Game of Life

Terri Marie

Your Inner Cheerleader, by Terri Marie

Library and Archives Cataloguing in Publication;

Marie, Terri
      Your Inner Cheerleader / by Terri Marie.

ISBN 978-0-943477-27-5

    1. Self-actualization (Psychology) 2. Self-help techniques.
    3. Success.

I. Title.

BF637.S4M354 2005   158.1   C2005-902930-7

Dedication

To Brooke, my amazing daughter
and Roy and Rosita, my beautiful parents.
You are all my favorite cheerleaders
in the Big Game of Life.

CONTENTS

APPENDIX

WITH GRATITUDE

Ironically, you need a lot of encouragement to write a book about encouragement, because when you decide to take on the challenge, life sends you plenty of lessons. Lessons designed to teach you how to teach others how to encourage themselves. If you think that's a mouthful, you should have seen the lessons! These lessons came through the guise of "problems" that had to be overcome. Luckily, I was helped by the following great "cheerleaders" whom I would like to thank.

My Own Team of Cheerleaders:

Jack Nichols - You were the spark. I cannot thank you enough. Your advice with the beginning stages of this book helped make it happen.

Roy and Seedy Thorson - Anytime I called and needed encouragement, which was often, I got it.

Brooke - How wonderful to have such a daughter! I will always be cheering for you.

Jody – My sweet sister, thank you for encouraging me to give the speech which became this book.

Lynn and Butch - God's cheerleaders.

Fawn O'Connor - Your cheery messages were always divinely guided.

Joe Vitale - Your love for this book helped immensely. I love you. Thank you.

Brian Adams - You demonstrated the high value of entertaining people and letting people leave your presence feeling lighter.

George Maier - For showing me the lightness of a writer, thank you.

John Harricharan – Thank you so much for your great help and friendship.

John Assaraf - You pushed me over the edge so that I COULD DO IT!

Irvin Kershner – For your belief in me, for your passion for the best in life and for your wisdom when I needed it, thank you.

Dottie Walters – You believed in me. Thank you Dottie my friend.

Ted Nicholas –Thank you for your warm support.

Robert Allen – For your yell of delight upon seeing this completed book.

Alfred Herzing – You told me one of the most valuable pieces of information in my life and helped prepare me to speak.

Glynis McCants – Thank you for the encouragement.

Mira Pastermac - You helped me get through the challenge – sometimes with a cup of tea and a bowl of spaghetti. You are a true friend.

Ginger and Ron Albrecht - You helped me get to a place that always "cheers me up." I am deeply grateful to you for that.

Karen Goodbody, Betsy and Steve D'Arca - For the wonderful places to rest.

To the wonderful speakers at Speakers Bureau of Orange County - Thank you for your gifts as we have learned and grown together.

To those many fine authors who have lit a spot in my soul with their words, I deeply thank you.

So many people have helped me get to this point in my life game by their gracious gifts of love and time. I am eternally grateful. To all those dear ones who helped in any way with this book, from my fellow speakers to the many people I called for advice, permission and clarification, bless you.

And above all, none of this would have been written without the inspiration, guidance and trust from my great Creator. I am profoundly grateful for the opportunity to write this book. Thank you.

FOREWORD

I love cheerleaders. Not only because they are usually beautiful, upbeat, energetic, and positive, but because their energy is so contagious. Hang around cheerleaders and you *want* to get out there and win the game. You can't stay in a room with cheerleaders and feel depressed or stay inactive. It seems like a violation of a law of physics.

The beauty of Terri Marie's book is that it trains *you* to be your own cheerleader. Imagine the possibilities: Instead of waiting for the phone to ring, or a friend to come over, or to get a date with a cheerleader, you turn inside and find that voice that says, "You can do it! Yes, YOU!"

Too often people listen to that little voice of doubt within themselves. Oh, you know the one. It tells you that you can't succeed, or you're too young, too old, too fat, too thin, too smart, too dumb, etc. It's the voice whispering in your head right now, "Is this book for me? I'm different and not everything works for me."

That's not your cheerleader.

Terri Marie reveals a way for you to develop, own, and have push-button ready, your own cheerleader. It's a new voice in your head. It's a new you. It's the you that believes in you, your dreams, and your goals. It's your authentic self. It's more akin to your spirit.

This is why I love Terri Marie's book, her, and her message. It gives you the power to fulfill your dreams. It plugs you into the source of magic and miracles.

You don't need to be around cheerleaders. You just need to be one. This book shows you how.

Hip-Hip-Hooray!

Joe Vitale; Author, "The Attractor Factor"
www.mrfire.com

The most powerful words in the English language
are the ones you say to yourself.
Naomi Judd

PREFACE

The golden opportunity you are seeking is in yourself.
it is not in your environment;
it is not in luck or chance, or the help of others;
it is in yourself alone.
Orison Swett Marden

WHAT IF THERE WAS A WAY to give yourself access to unlimited energy - the special energy you need to succeed in your life? What if there were a way to greatly increase your chances to "win" the kind of life you want? What if your only investment was time, sometimes as little as 30 seconds of your time, before you took an important action? Or a minute or two each morning? What if you could say something to yourself that would change, in a positive way, the things that will happen in your life? Would you do it?

There exists an amazing power within you. If you tap into this inner power, you will reach a source that is always with you. It is always positive. It always knows which encouragement you need to accomplish what you intend to do with your life.

I call this the INNER CHEERLEADER. Everyone has this power, and I will show you how to access that part of yourself that knows success and knows how to win. We will go through the game together using the Inner Cheerleader as a guide. A cheerleader attitude will get you through the tough times - times when the weaker parts of you want to leave. Bring on the Inner Cheerleader and watch what happens. Success will start to dance around you. When you want to chicken out, the Inner Cheerleader will turn the chicken part of you into a phoenix. When you believe your life or situation is hopeless, you too can rise from the ashes - a new, beautiful and mysterious creation who can cheer you through those challenging little games you face within the Big Game of Life.

Some people think cheerleaders are only motivators. That is just not true. While motivation is a part of what they do, a cheerleader has to take massive action to become a cheerleader and to remain one. Actions like practicing skills, learning to stretch the body and mind past previous limits, polishing communication skills, developing teamwork and being able to pull something up from within themselves to lead large groups of people, even and especially when the cheerleader does not feel like it.

There are a lot of business skills that cheerleaders learn: planning, creating and practicing the cheers, designing stunning halftime displays, scheduling workouts, coordinating pep rallies, making banners and working with the community. All of these require plenty of time, effort and a good head on their cheery shoulders.

Some of the ideas presented here are truly motivational, and motivation is one key to your success. But make no mistake. You will have to take action, plan and deliver something valuable to the world if you want to succeed. And a cheerleader knows how to do that.

Success is beyond motivation. It is transformational. It is a deep knowing that you deserve and have the ability to live the life you desire. What you say to yourself and how you cheer for or against yourself are the most important actions you can take to determine your amount of success in the game of life. The Inner Cheerleader will transform your life.

Would you like to have your own cheerleader? You already do, for we all have a cheerleader inside us that we can bring to life. Once you "develop" that cheerleader within, it will always be there for you. You will have built a hero.

There is no time like the present to start! Come with me as we explore how you can access your Inner Cheerleader who will drive you and guide you to the success you've always wanted in life. Let's get started. Let's reveal that cheerleader within you.

INTRODUCTION

When you cannot get a compliment any other way,

pay yourself one.

Mark Twain

Everyone has these cheerleader voices that speak to us,

"Wow! You did it!"

Robert Allen

YOUR INTRODUCTION TO "THE GAME"

We are not in the regular game of life anymore.
We are in the play-offs.
Terri Marie

It is for people like you that I wrote this book. If you've had some bad luck, if things are not going right in your life, I am here to tell you that time is over. It is time for you to win. It is your turn for success. That is why I'm glad you are reading this book. I want you to win.

There is something inside you that wants you to succeed. There is a tool that will make you more successful at reaching your goals. Something that can be trained, developed and used to help you succeed. An Inner Cheerleader. Yes, you have one. Have you ever cheered a child to win at a ball game, or encouraged a spouse to go for a dream, or uplifted a friend's spirit when they were feeling down? Then you have been a cheerleader. You can use the same talents you use to encourage others, to motivate yourself. This book will teach you how to find and develop your Inner Cheerleader through the techniques that have worked in my life and in the lives of many other cheerleaders. It will help you become your own hero.

You'll learn some strategies that cheerleaders use, so that you can bring out the hero that exists within you. You will begin to think and encourage yourself like a cheerleader does. I will share some cheers that have worked well for me. Cheers to prime the pump until your Inner Cheerleader takes over on its own.

Every one of us talks to ourselves, usually all day long. Sometimes all night long. Did you ever see the movie where the actor can "hear" all the people's thoughts? Thoughts like "I wonder why he said that." "I'm late again." "Why did I eat so much?"

We all self-talk. The part of us that listens does not always choose the best messages to pay attention to. However, there is a part of you that longs to encourage you. Once you know how to recognize and develop this internal resource, you can use this valuable ally for your own success.

Let me tell you why Inner Cheerleading is such an effective form of self-motivation.

- Cheers work well anywhere and for any situation
- You always have access to them
- You can create them yourself to suit the occasion
- No one else has to know about them
- THEY WORK!

You have an outer cheerleader and an Inner Cheerleader. You are other people's outer cheerleader, and they are yours. But others are not always available. Your Inner Cheerleader is. Sometimes others give you the motivation *they* want you to have. Your Inner Cheerleader can give you exactly the encouragement *you* need. Your Inner Cheerleader does not have to be overpowering, but it does have to be strong. Stronger than any negative self-talk you may have. Leadership is "outward" focused. Inner Cheerleading is **Inner Leadership.**

I used to believe that others who were successful had advantages I didn't have, like lots of money or someone who had encouraged them and pushed them along. Some "motivator" who told them they could succeed. Perhaps this motivator even scheduled their life or constantly reminded, organized and led them to success. A success guide.

One day it hit me. I was looking out "there" for someone to make me successful, and blaming the world when I was not. Bingo! Success was inside me. I was the one who needed to guide myself, encourage myself and lead myself to the successes I knew were waiting for me in life, the same way I cheered for a team to win back when I was a cheerleader. It is a crossroads of personal responsibility that every successful person comes to. It is the decision to create the life you want, taking full personal responsibility for every one of your choices.

My Inner Cheerleading Moment

Sometimes opportunities come without warning. They fly briefly into your life. If you do not recognize and hold onto them, they fly away.

This book was first a speech. In order to qualify for The Speakers Bureau of Orange County, California, I had to write and give a twenty-minute speech. Several good ideas presented themselves, but nothing was long enough. Then the opportunity came, although I did not recognize it at first. One busy week, five people from my past called me. They all had major emotional challenges, and all of them needed a lot of encouragement. This was really strange, and I was thinking, "Why all these calls? Why now, in such a short time frame?"

I finally asked the big question: "What did I give them that they needed?" In other words, what specifically were they looking for from me? I knew I had helped them, but I did not fully realize what I had done or the power of it at the time.

The big question simmered in my mind for a few hours. I was lying in my hammock relaxing later in the afternoon and Eureka! The answer came in a flash. *I was encouraging them. I was CHEERING THEM UP!*

It was then that I realized I usually cheered for everyone except myself. It was a huge awakening for me when I saw this; a major revelation. For most of my life I used the outer cheerleader; cheering for friends or family to go for dreams, to make it through life's dark tunnels, or to encourage the weary and scared. But that day in the hammock, I realized I was not using the cheerleader to help *me* succeed. I was not taking advantage of my own Inner Cheerleader. That is when my life changed. It started to work.

It was clear to me that the lives of my friends who needed cheering up might be better if they could find their own personal Inner Cheerleader to help them each day. And if so many of my friends needed a self-motivator, perhaps that Inner Cheerleader would be valuable to others as well.

That is when I decided to write a guide to creating your own Inner Cheerleader. A simple plan about how you can develop this Inner Cheerleader and create the success you want. In looking at my experiences as a cheerleader from a new perspective, I wrote about the cheering strategies that have helped me succeed in life. You, too, can use these strategies, which include some cheers to help you get started until your own Inner Cheerleader takes over.

We all want to win at the great game of life. We are all playing the BIG Game. I want to help you play at your highest level and enjoy it. Enjoy it for what it is; something beautiful, exciting, sometimes heartbreaking and extraordinarily valuable.

Because everyone needs to encourage themselves to succeed, why not have fun doing it? Being a cheerleader was a fun and wonderful experience. It was a great feeling gazing out at the squad, all dressed in bright uniforms, looking up at hundreds of smiling faces in the stands, excitement in the air and glittering pompoms swishing around in rhythmic patterns. We saw that huge empty field about to be filled with energy. It was incredible! It was the energy of moving, dancing, jumping and cheering, so full of life that set me on a path that still leads my way many years later.

Do you have any letters, notes or emails you save because they really pick you up? What if you sent yourself one of those letters? Wouldn't you feel great reading, "You are a fantastic person!" or "You are special!"? Sometimes you need encouragement but there is no one around who can or will encourage you. How would your life change if you could get the encouragement you need whenever you need it, from a source that is always with you?

In World War II, the cheering slogan "We can do it!" was placed everywhere to encourage and cheer the country on. While the soldiers overseas could not see those signs, I believe that they could feel the support coming from the home front. Be that support system for yourself, and you can make it through anything life throws at you.

Cheerleading is Not For Wimps or Sissies

Was the first cheerleader named Jack...or Jill? It was Jack! Jack Campbell, a University of Minnesota medical student, became the first cheerleader in the late 1800s when he jumped in front of a crowd and yelled for victory. He became the first official "cheerleader."

Let's go back to the first cheer. The first group of unofficial "cheerleaders" was from Princeton and they were all men. Back in the late 1800s, when Junior went to football games on his horse (instead of in his Porsche!), there were cheerleaders.

Women did not take over the ranks of cheerleading until WWII when most of the men went off to war.

Way back in the 1870s, Princeton organized the first pep club,
we presume to celebrate their tremendous wealth.
www.SOYOUWANNABE.com

The Cheer That Didn't Catch On

The University of Minnesota was having a horrible football season back in the late 1800s. A professor developed and presented his scientific theory; namely, that the collective stimuli of several hundred students sending focused and positive energy in a team's direction could help them win. His talk ended with a rousing cry and a cheer. The game came and the Minnesota Gophers got clobbered 28-0. The cheer did not work. It could have been because it did not roll off the tongue very well...

GO TO MADISON, GO TO MADISON
APPLY THE SUMMATION OF THE STIMULI

I do not think I would say that little charmer more than once, either. I think the professor came up with a great line for a sci-fi movie: "CAPTAIN, APPLY THE SUMMATION OF THE STIMULI, AND HURRY!" His concept, good. The content was not exactly motivational.

Some Famous Cheerleaders

Many famous people got their start as cheerleaders. Do you think that is a coincidence?

- U.S. President Dwight D. Eisenhower
- Actor Jimmy Stewart
- Actor Kirk Douglas
- Actress Meryl Streep
- Actress Raquel Welch
- Actor John Wayne *

All right, John Wayne was not really a cheerleader in school, but do you think he ever encouraged a fellow actor? You bet! In fact, he encouraged Kirk Douglas (the real cheerleader) when Kirk was thinking about taking a role as a bad guy. Wayne said, "Kirk, we don't play those kinds of roles. We only play the heroes."

*See the appendix for more famous cheerleaders

Do you play the hero for yourself? Why not? You can.

Was a basketball player or football player ever President? NO! It was a cheerleader. Who better to organize and lead the masses?

Many of you are going it alone these days. As entrepreneurs, you need to motivate yourself with a good pep talk.

An Inner Cheerleader can do that. Don't be a "fear" leader. When a cheerleader asks, "Do you want to win?" the only answer she is looking for is "Yes!"

If you had a cheer for everything you do, then you would be more successful at everything you do. When you cheer, you are focusing energy. We all have this cheerleader inside, this internal encourager, but we rarely use it. Why not? It is a FUN, yet profound way to teach yourself how to succeed.

Picture this: a young man or woman, fearful to begin a new journey in life, is approached by an older, wiser person, whom they greatly admire.

Every morning the wise person looks this young person in the eye, and with deep love and conviction says, "You can do this. You are strong enough. You are courageous enough. You have all the tools you need to succeed. I believe in you. I believe in you completely. I have faith in you. You are capable of this and much more." Every morning the wise person comes by, smiles, and repeats this message or the one most urgently needed by the young person. Do you think that this young person's life would change? Indeed it would.

That wise person is you. Within you. You can bring yourself to the dwelling place of this part of yourself. This is the domain of love, where "encouragement" (*coeur* - the heart) lives and can provide you with the guidance, the motivation, and most of all the belief that you are here to succeed. Your dreams were put inside you for a reason, so you could uncover them and give them to the world.

I believe that each day you must do something to encourage yourself, just like you need to eat every day for nourishment and exercise for your physical health. Whether you do this program or a different one, choose some way to consistently provide self-motivation. It is important that it comes from you, from within. That will cause huge, positive changes in your life, from a source that can never be taken away.

You win the game by being the best you possible. The full potential *you*. The *you* that you love. The *you* that the world loves. You become the hero of your own game.

How Do You Develop an Inner Cheerleader?

How can you nurture that Inner Cheerleader of yours? What do cheerleaders do that you can do to encourage yourself to win? Would you like to know how you can create excitement in your life, your work, or your business? As a businesswoman I am giving you ways to create that Inner Cheerleader, so that by the end of this book, you have some strategies for being a strong self-supporter. You will become a self-directed leader – your own hero. These are the skills I use that have helped me most in life, and I would like to share them with you. Use this book as a guide to do the cheers that will bring you the successes that have your name on them.

First you will learn how to develop your Inner Cheerleader, then when and how to use your own Inner Cheerleader to create the success you want.

You will read about the values of an Inner Cheerleader, what to do before, during and after the game and what the game teaches Inner Cheerleaders about life. If you want to, you can later skim the strategies, or go to the back of the book where they are listed as a refresher. You now can have a great Inner Cheerleader working for you!

Come with me.

Let's go back to when I was a cheerleader...

> *Stand on the sidelines of a football game on a crisp autumn night. Smell the rich aroma of burning leaves drifting across the hazy autumn sky. Look out over that football field, across the green glittery turf. Golden helmets bounce and clash in the crisp black air. Giant shoulders flex in the lights. You can hear the excitement of the crowd behind you swell like an ocean. There is an air of anticipation all around. Your heart is absolutely overflowing.*

This is the feeling the Inner Cheerleader creates.

CONGRATULATIONS FOR TAKING A LOOK
GO ON TO THE CHEERS – YOU'VE STARTED THE BOOK!
NOW YOU CAN CHEER FOR YOURSELF – HIP HOORAY!
IF Y OU BEGIN NOW, YOU'LL BE AMAZED EVERY DAY
STEP BY STEP, YOUR DREAMS WILL APPEAR
WHEN Y OU BEGIN RIGHT NOW, TO LEARN HOW TO CHEER!

LET'S GO!

Chapter 1

THE CHEERING SECTION

The truth is we all talk to ourselves.
We just need to get better at it.
Thom Rutledge

BE OF GOOD CHEER

Be of good cheer...Remember, no effort that we make to
attain something beautiful is ever lost.
Helen Keller

Cheering for yourself is not the only thing you will need to do to achieve success, but it is a critical part of success, just as taking appropriate action at the right time is. Just as learning the skills you need to succeed is. Just as getting out and circulating in the world is. Think of success as a suitcase for a trip you are taking. You will need a passport, clothes, money, etc. Cheers are one of those important things to pack into your suitcase on your trip to success.

In this section are some descriptions of what makes a good cheer, and also a few cheers to get you going. Remember, the goal is to create your own cheers that will lead you to the specific successes you desire. For every thing that is wrong in your life, there is a cheer that will correct it. For every dream in your heart, there is a cheer that will seduce it. The following cheers will help you get started. Have some fun with them. Make up cheers that motivate and encourage you. And then DO them.

THE 5 QUALITIES OF A GOOD CHEER

- Motivates
- Raises self-esteem
- Describes the action necessary to win
- Focuses on the goals
- Programs the beliefs *you* choose into your life

There are several pointers throughout the book that are especially potent. Here they are.

I CAN DO IT!

Perhaps the most powerful cheer of all is "I CAN DO IT!" This is a cheer to add to your belief system if you want to have or achieve anything. This is a BE-lief. You must BE first, then the having and achieving naturally result. Results must follow, because this is such a strong program. If you have this belief, you will not have the following belief, which, I believe, is perhaps the cheer that creates the least personal power.

"I can't _____."

(fill in the blank with your verb of choice)

I told my daughter the four-letter word "can't" was not allowed in our home. She grew up believing that anything is possible and has achieved amazing success in her young life. Because there is no room for the "can't" word in her mind, she is an excellent problem-solver.

Author Joe Vitale was on a panel with other successful business people and was asked the question, "You are successful, but that's because you're special. What about the rest of us?" I will never forget Joe's response: "*Anyone* can be successful. It's almost an insult to our Creator to believe that we aren't capable."

Most people hear someone successful tell them, "You can do it!" and they think, "Yes. You can, but *I* can't." All BIG thinkers and most successful people know that YOU CAN do it too, for they were once unsuccessful.

If you believe you CAN, you WILL and you DO. Add this cheer to your repertoire now. Use it often.

I CAN DO IT!
YOU CAN DO IT!
WE CAN DO IT!

I psyched myself up with positive talk.
'Stay focused but enjoy the experience.

You can do this.' I repeated this over and over.
I needed to be in great shape mentally and physically
to project myself the most effectively.
Phyllis George

DO THE THIRTY-SECOND CHEER

Thirty seconds before an event take affirmative action. Cheer for yourself and the result you wish. A commercial takes just 30 seconds and uses powerful messages that "encourage" a lot of people to buy things. Before you do something, take a short "cheer" break. Like a commercial, do a cheer for the success you want. Then watch the surprising results.

Here is a quick example: Let's say you have a special call to make that you are nervous about. Before the call, cheer for thirty seconds for the motivation you need and the result you want. You could say, "I am SO confident, they are going to feel it through the phone! They are going to LOVE hearing from me," "I'm smiling because I KNOW I am destined for success." Do this for 30 seconds. FEEL it. This also works before you open an important email, before you open an important door or even open the mail. You *can* influence the outcome.

Cheer for your new belief for 30 seconds. You will make a huge impact in your life.

ADD A PHYSICAL MOVEMENT TO YOUR CHEERS

Adding movement adds energy. It "moves" things. It is helpful if that "thing" moved is yourself. By creating movement, you start things in motion. It gives added impact to your cheers, your affirmations. One simple movement is to raise one hand at a time in the air, repeating your cheer. This is very energizing. Another is to raise your right leg across your body and touch your left elbow to the right knee. Alternate with your left leg and your right elbow. Do this for 30 seconds with each cheer you do. Simple – yes, but BIG Results.

The famous movie *Seven Samurai* by Akira Kurosawa has a profound scene where the well-outnumbered farmers are being invaded by fierce bandits. The Samurai were told by the Grandfather of the village to hire Samurai warriors to help defend them. As the dawn of the big battle came, the makeshift army was very scared. The Samurai knew they had to change that feeling or the farmers were doomed. The Samurai told the farmers, who were hiding, to cheer. "Come out all of you. Now, yell," they said. A huge cry arose among the farmers. The entire energy changed. It would not have changed without that cheer, without the belief of their leaders and their determination to give their all to their goal.

Can you imagine the Samurai cheering without lifting their swords, stakes or whatever else was at hand? The Samurai used their whole bodies to cheer. You must infuse every cell with your intent, your goal and cheer for it with the amazing body you have. Your body is full of information. Move it around, like the Seven Cheering Samurai who took on a very large and most frightening goal...and succeeded.

USE THE REPLAY EFFECTIVELY

*Stop the habits of replaying past failures and instead
purposefully replay our successes in our minds,
which over time will enhance our self-image.*
Charles Manz

Cheers are most effective if you replay them. Over and over. Of course, make sure you are doing the "right" cheers to get you to your desired results. Replaying a negative cheer or what went wrong during the game is not productive. Learning is. Replay what is right, what is already working. Figure out by replaying your best moments, how you felt, what you did and what caused those great results. But most importantly, create good cheers, and replay them and replay them....

DO THE OPPOSITE CHEER

If you are feeling anything but absolute clarity, any little touch of fear inside, ask what you are afraid of. Then do the opposite cheer. You have just shoved fear off-stage and taken over the act. For instance, when you call and ask for a sale, if the "They won't buy from me" *fear* thought comes in, send in the "I am a great salesperson and I sell a great product" thought. Send in the "They are lucky to hear from me" *cheer* thought. These powerful little cheers will change the energy from fear to cheer. This is a major point. Doing the opposite of what has not worked for you often DOES work.

DO A CHEER
THAT IS OPPOSITE OF YOUR FEAR

And remember throughout the book...

IT IS JUST A GAME

Business is a game. You are already on a team.
That's it. Either you play or you don't.
If you're interested in succeeding,
playing the game will help
you achieve your goals.
Gail Evans

Have fun, especially when you remember that it is a game you choose to play. Play well. Play your best. Enjoy it. When an actor goes on stage, he creates the role he plays. The script contains the lines to be read, but the actor brings the emotions and the "character" to it. He can play the role however he and the director choose. He creates. He has fun.

That is how life is.

We have scripts, but most of them are unconscious. Luckily we can get a different script and play a different role we might enjoy more.

I did a documentary on the Utah Shakespearean Festival in Cedar City, Utah. The designer went to get me a costume for the show. I wanted her to bring me an elegant costume, something refined and royal. Instead she came back with a "wench" costume. Actually it looked kind of like a flower child costume. The costume designer said to me, "You don't want to be a 'lady.' They can't do anything but stand around and act royal. A wench can have fun."

Although I was initially disappointed, she was right. I played the part. I was able to be light-hearted. I danced, got carried by a king, teased by a troubadour and kissed on the hand by a charming child. I had a Shakespearean ball! The costume and the "role" were given to me, but I got into the costume, enjoyed the role and created the fun. It made for a much better documentary.

If you remember nothing else from this book, remember the various cheers found throughout this chapter:

- I CAN DO IT!
- DO THE THIRTY-SECOND CHEER
- ADD A PHYSICAL MOVEMENT TO YOUR CHEERS
- USE THE REPLAY EFFECTIVELY
- DO THE OPPOSITE CHEER
- IT IS JUST A GAME

These are the primary cheers, the foundation and the base. If you start with just those cheers, they will add a huge boost to your life. If you can add an "I CAN DO IT!" attitude, that alone will make your game more successful. Much more. Believing in yourself that strongly will work miracles. If you are looking for more magic in your life, here it is.

Successful people rarely tell you
'You can't do it.'
Only unsuccessful people tell you that.
Robert Allen

When I do any cheer I make sure I have:

1. **High energy:** a personal pep rally OR a deeply felt emotion, which contains very intense, focused energy as in looking in a mirror.
2. **A visual image**: as if it is happening right now and I am taking part in it.
3. **A release** - a non-attachment: as in watching a movie. Once you have finished the movie, you go on to other things.

HIGH ENERGY

High energy can be plenty of excitement, which doesn't necessarily require yelling, but bright energy. It can also be energy that moves you. When I stayed at a friend's home, I went into her bathroom. Something about the room, the light, who knows, just hit me. When I saw my reflection in her mirror, I felt a deep connection to myself that I knew would intensify any "cheering" I did. I spent about 15 minutes "programming" in all sorts of good stuff. I could feel myself changing. When you have something like this happen - and you will - use it to your advantage. It may even be higher energy than jumping around with pompoms - but probably not as much fun! I use both methods.

USE EMOTIONAL INTENSITY

To succeed at life, you must visualize and create emotional excitement about what it is you want. Despite our stereotypes, men are much better at creating this energy than women are. That is one reason why men have traditionally been more successful than women. Women are taught to suppress the emotions of excitement and express milder emotions like concern, caring etc. Men are taught to play sports, which are HIGH intensity. They are used to really expressing their feelings while playing that sport. Watch football players and see how carried away they get emotionally when a touchdown is made. The players all hug each other with HIGH, HIGH intensity. They yell. They really get caught up in the game. Do you see women do this? Not as much. Men use that intensity to succeed at business because they already have that "excitement" muscle developed. Many men are trained from early on to have these high, intense feeling experiences.

Imagine a young man surfing. Alone with nature, the ocean's power, waves crashing around him. The young man must match the "intensity" of the ocean with his own force. So many more men are actually better prepared to reach the passion required that is necessary for success. Men were the first cheerleaders... but women learn fast.

A VISUAL IMAGE

See the most powerful moment of your life when you cheer. Feel that feeling and put it with your cheer. Absorb that feeling into the cheer. Infuse it with visual power.

I used an image of my beautiful, sweet dog in front of me when I was auditioning for a television show. She always cheered me up and I was able to smile and forget that I was nervous when I imagined looking at her.

THE RELEASE

Release your cheer after you have done it. Know that it is planted now. Trust that it will bear fruit. You can do your cheer over and over, daily if you wish, but release it each time.

Every time you throw a ball, you release it. You can throw it again, but first you must release it. Feel the emotion with your cheer and then feel your heart open and just let it go.

Here is your starting line-up of cheers. The following are catchy little cheers that can help you when you need a boost. Give that boost to yourself now. There's no excuse anymore.

CHEERS FOR DIFFERENT OCCASIONS

Cheering Up Cheers

I AM GREAT AND THAT'S A FACT
I DESERVE A BIG PAT ON THE BACK
The message: **I have what it takes to succeed**

Cheers For Trust

I AM GREAT, I CAN SUCCEED
LIFE WILL MEET MY EVERY NEED
The message: **I can have what I ask for.**

Cheers For Motivation

KEEP ON GOING, I KNOW I'LL MAKE IT
PUSH RIGHT NOW...EVEN IF I HAVE TO FAKE IT
The message: **I was created for success. I can win**

EACH STEP I TAKE
BRINGS ME NEAR
TO THE LIFE I WANT
THAT'S WHY I CHEER
The message: **I can do it**
Cheers To Go Through Fear

You cannot avoid fear. You go through it.
WE ALL HAVE FEAR
I DON'T KEEP IT NEAR
I PUSH RIGHT THROUGH
AND MAKE THINGS NEW
The message: **I am safe**

These are just a few cheers to jump-start your Inner Cheerleader. However, the most important cheers you do will be those that you get an "insight" to do. For instance, you realize you have been procrastinating. A good cheer for changing procrastination is "I do what I say I'm going to do!" Make up your own cheers to help you with your challenges. Repeating a cheer often and seeing yourself accomplishing it in your mind drives that cheer deeply into your subconscious. It changes you. You determine the change you want and do the cheer to create it. Have fun with it. Change is normal but it doesn't have to be hard. You can make it fun.

Here are some of my favorite cheers, cheers that I have used to create more success in my life. Many of them are so potent for me that I still use them every day.

I CAN WIN!
I DESERVE SUCCESS!

I MAKE GREAT DECISIONS!

I CAN HAVE WHAT I ASK FOR!

I AM VERY FOCUSED!

I ACHIEVE THE GOALS I SET!

I CLEARLY SEE FANTASTIC SOLUTIONS AND INSIGHTS!

I ACHIEVE GREAT RESULTS WITH MINIMUM EFFORT!

I DO WHAT I SAY I'M GOING TO DO!

SUCCESS IS MY BIRTHRIGHT!

TODAY IS THE BEST DAY OF MY LIFE!

I have also borrowed some powerful cheers that work for me. Here's one from author and friend John Harricharan.

An endless avalanche of abundance now pours down upon me.

And when I walk, I tell myself this "cheer" that always lifts me up.

God loves me today and always and he shows me that love through abundance and happiness. Today is the best day of my life.

There were mornings I had to force myself to do the cheers, because I didn't FEEL like it. That's exactly when I needed them most. So I did force myself. Then I really got into doing the cheers. You know what? I FELT better - a lot better! I had more energy. Even my face looked better. Sometimes you just have to say to yourself, "I know you don't want to do this right now (acknowledge) but we are going to anyway (action)."

THE POWER OF THE CHEER

The two most important times to do your cheers for the life changes you want are right after you wake up and right before you go to sleep. In addition to the "Magic Moment" talked about later, these are times the mind is more receptive to change.

A husband used to come into the bedroom as his wife was lying in bed ready to fall asleep, when her mind was very receptive to suggestion, whether positive or negative. He would start a fight and yell horrible things at her and then leave to go sleep in another room. Powerful, powerful, negative conditioning! It took a huge amount of reconditioning for this woman to overcome all that emotional abuse - but if she did it - so can you!

You can use these critical receptive times to program your Inner Cheerleader with POSITIVE CHEERS. In the same way that negative cheers work so well to keep us down, positive ones work wonders to cheer us "up" - UP in success, UP in happiness and UP in life. Success can't wait to see you when you cheer for it so enthusiastically. It is your birthright.

Like positive encouragement, cheers can help everyone. But what if you, the Cheerer, don't have a support system for those words to land on, to adhere to? Inner Cheerleaders need a belief system that, like the crowd in the stadium, yells back, "YES!"

YOUR VALUES GIVE CLUES
LIKE READING THE NEWS
THEY SERVE AS THE HEADLINE
IN THE LIFE STORY YOU DEFINE

Chapter 2

VALUES

*Values are like fingerprints. Nobody's are the same
but you leave 'em all over everything you do.*
Elvis Presley

If you change your values your beliefs must change.
Bill Harris

www.yourinnercheerleader.com

VALUES

To create your Inner Cheerleader, let's start with some basic values that most cheerleaders have. To create success, Inner Cheerleaders do these things, they think these things, they know these things and they believe these things.

1. BELIEVE YOU CAN WIN

All personal breakthroughs begin with a change in beliefs.
Anthony Robbins

As cheerleaders, we always believed our team had a chance, even when we played the team with the football player called "King Kong." Cheerleaders know that what you tell the crowd matters. Did you ever hear the following cheer?

"Why do you have the ball?
You're not going to win after all!"

Of course not! Not from a true cheerleader. But we have all heard someone tell us a form of that cheer sometime in our lives. Maybe it even was yourself! Someone might have told you that you could not do something. Did you believe them? Do you still believe them? Did someone tell you that you could not sing? Do they know more about you than you do? I don't think so.

Until I was in my 40s I never wrote a note of music. All of a sudden one day, I sat at the piano and started to play a beautiful little melody. I thought it was a fluke. A very nice fluke, but I never expected another song. Yet another day, another song was in my fingers. I just had to move them on the piano. Earlier in my life I had been told I was not a musician. That is what I believed until my fingers told me the truth, and I have believed them ever since.

Belief in yourself must come before accomplishment, not after.
Joan Lunden

You, too, can create powerful and positive beliefs to help you succeed. One way to help cheer yourself on and push out the negative beliefs is to use a list of affirmations that represent the success you want. Cheerleaders use positive statements that are short, sweet and in the present - an affirmation.* An affirmation is not airy-fairy. When you use an affirmation with strong, positive feelings, like a cheerleader does, real power is created.
*There is a special section on the power of affirmations in Appendix A.

FIRST AND 10
DO IT AGAIN!

In business you can use:
WAY TO GO!
YOU MADE THE CALL!
YOU'RE NUMBER ONE!

You are in a meeting. The first point goes your way. The "fearleader" thinks, "Uh oh, they are going to want the next point." The cheerleader thinks, "First and 10. Do it again!"

In your business is your cheer, "They won't buy so why even try"? You better pick a new cheer. How about this one? "They can't wait to hear from me!"

GET LOUD
GET CLEAR

My doctor saved my life, not by giving me a pill, but by spending an hour patiently talking with me, telling me with utmost conviction that I would get through a terrible crisis. I choose to believe him. And I did get through that extraordinarily difficult challenge, although it was not easy. His words at that moment were stronger than any medicine on earth. Many doctors use words in the opposite manner and unfortunately some patients believe them.

Have a YOU CAN DO IT! Attitude

We are the ones that sell our beliefs short by refusing to act on them and stick by them through thick and thin.
Dorothy Carnegie

To break through a barrier in your life you will have rise to a new level. This is how you will reach the success you want. If you do not have some barriers, your goals are not big enough. Your barrier will have some fear around it. Naturally, barriers feel a little scary and many people never attempt to get past them. Confronting a barrier is like walking into a dark room and feeling afraid. But, remember, you have the ability to turn on the light in that room. Cheers can help you do this. You are the one who put up the barrier as a way of dealing with a challenge in the past.

But to grow, you need to go past the boundary that you initially set to protect yourself. Don't hold on to your good work from the past if it is no longer serving you.

In a seminar I was once challenged to break a board with the palm of my hand. The board looked pretty darn thick to me and I thought, "I am not a karate expert." Yet I got up to do it when it was my turn. *Slam!* My hand hit the vertical board. The board remained in one piece. My hand smarted and felt like it was broken in two. *Slam!* I hit it again. My hand smarted even more. The group asked me if I wanted to give up and break it with my foot instead. I said "No way!"

A second way to break the board with my fist was suggested, horizontally - like the karate experts do. I tried that. At first I tried to do it too fast. It seemed like there were a million people all yelling at me with different instructions. After one attempt, they again suggested I just break it with my foot. Then the leader of the group bent down, looked me directly in the eye and said, *"Terri Marie, you can do this!"* Within his eye contact somehow there was a message that I got. I *knew* I could break that board. I had them set it back up and slammed my fist down. This time the board flew apart. And it did not hurt.

Look yourself in the eye and say, "{YOUR NAME}, you can do this."

I believe the statement "You can do it!" said with belief and felt with passion is one of the most powerful on the planet.

Have you put this powerful cheer into your repertoire yet? Add it now.

I CAN DO IT!

Or do you have this belief?

I CAN'T DO IT
I NEVER WILL
SO WHY EVEN TRY
'CUZ I'M OVER THE HILL

If you are over the hill, sing *Hallelujah!* You have already done the hard part - the climbing. Now it's clear sailing. Now is the fun part!

Dorothy, in *The Wizard of Oz,* used affirmations to reach her goal of getting back to Kansas. "There's no place like home. There's no place like home," she said over and over. Glenda, The Good Witch, knew what Dorothy needed to do to get back home. Repeat that dream of yours, or that change you want to make, with conviction and with the power of your word, and see where it takes you.

WHAT YOU BELIEVE IS WHAT YOU RECEIVE
BELIEVE YOU CAN WIN!

A little poem about beliefs:

Believe you can do it
And there's nothing to it
Because within your brain
Exists every possible gain
And everything that ever will be
Was first a belief in you and in me

2. CHEERLEADING IS ADDICTING

Cheers are Catchy like a Song with a Hook

Once you start cheering, you will not want to stop. Like a song that has a hook and stays in your head, you will be cheering all the time. This drives noncheerleaders crazy, but makes YOUR life a lot better and more successful.

One of the most effective ways to learn is "row, row, row your boat" learning. That is where you say a catchy phrase in a round-robin manner, similar to the song. Unfortunately you can be programming the wrong things, things that conflict with what you really want.

For example, let's say you have just made a silly mistake in front of your boss. You might find yourself saying, "Why didn't I just keep my mouth shut? I should have never spoken up? What did I think I was doing?" These are all variations on a theme with a common denominator: *fear*. Saying them over and over reinforces them in your mind so they actually have a better chance of happening again. On the other hand, even if you did make a fool of yourself, say instead, "Well, where did that come from? That sure was not my normal mode of operation but it was kind of funny, I suppose. Maybe I just made my boss feel quite smart. Maybe he needed that today. I think I will keep my eyes open for a possibility to really contribute today and see what happens." If you say something like that instead, you will open the door for circumstances from which you can choose again, better this time. Taking the same event but looking at it differently will give you a much better set of choices for your future.

Do you subconsciously sing "Tow, tow, tow your boat?" Don't drag it along! Use the "row, row, row your boat" technique to your advantage.

When you repeat a cheer or positive affirmation consistently and with high energy, that new "programming" burns itself into your mind.

Then your mind will run the new program instead of an old or inefficient one. That's how you create new successes. Cheers are done in the row, row, row your boat format. That is one of the reasons they are so powerful. They tap into the way your brain likes to learn - repetition, fun and high energy. The catchier you can make your cheers, the easier it will be for you to learn and accept the new attitude or belief you want to install. If you surround yourself with the success attitudes you desire, they will have to start manifesting in your life.

A few years back, I stayed in artist Jody Bergsma's painting room. It is in a loft upstairs in a little cabin on her estate. Surrounded by her paints and easels, all night long I dreamt in her painting style.

I saw painting after painting. It seemed as if those paintings lived in that room, as if those paintings were speaking to me. They came to life there, through Jody's talent. I believe there is an energy that stays on the football field or on the basketball court or in the bleachers that is latent. It is just waiting for cheerleaders to tap into it, open it up and use it. It is also there for you. The hero energy is all around us.

Picture an empty field full of possibilities, like in the movie *Field of Dreams*. There are energy exchanges during the game. Once you sense all that potential energy and taste it, you want more. Cheerleading is a good addiction.

CHEERS ARE GOOD ADDICTIONS
IF YOU SAY THEM WITH CONVICTION

3.   BE FLEXIBLE

Whatever is flexible and flowing will tend to grow.
Tao Te Ching

Cheerleaders are not just flexible in their joints. They are flexible in their attitude and in their decisions. They can change cheers fast. If a cheerleader starts doing one cheer and the other team gets the ball, she changes cheers. If her team steals it back, she changes cheers again. That is what the game is all about. The "as you go" goals can change. The focus is still the same. The big end goal, the touchdown, is the same.

The cheers change all throughout the game. Sometimes players get hurt. Sometimes they make fabulous catches or plays. Coaches call time-outs. No matter what happens in the game, focus on the goal and change your cheers to get there.

CHANGE CHEERS
TO CHANGE GEARS

4. CHEERLEADERS KNOW THEY ARE NOT THE TEAM

Sometimes things are beyond your control. If you have done your best and it still has not worked - let it go. Go on to the next game. Do not take it real personal. There is a lot of failure built into success. Do your best as a player and become even better.

The greatest athletes, those who get into the Hall of Fame, lose 5 out of 10 games. Yet they are considered great. Those players who lose 6 and a half times out of 10 are still thought of as great. They fail more than they succeed but they actually become the best out there because so many players fail even more. Or worse, they do not even try. Those who don't try usually end up in the Hall of Blame.

And the players who "*fail*" while trying to succeed often make millions a year. You cannot decide the outcome, but you can influence the game by your faith. You can influence the mood of the crowd around you.

When I interviewed James Roosevelt, the son of Franklin and Eleanor Roosevelt, I asked him whether Eleanor ever controlled the decisions of Franklin. "I can assure you she did not," he replied. Then he added, "But did she have influence on him? Absolutely!" You cannot control, but you CAN influence.

YOU ARE NOT THE TEAM
DO NOT GIVE UP ON YOUR DREAM

5. HAVE GREAT VALUES

Do what you feel in your heart to be right –
for you'll be criticized anyway.
Eleanor Roosevelt

Why do they call a group of cheerleaders a "squad"? A squad is a small group of people organized for a specific purpose, such as a police squad. Usually most people in a squad have similar values, values that serve their purpose.

Cheerleaders are looked up to in school. They have a responsibility to live a life of integrity. So, you too, can trust that Inner Cheerleader of yours not run around with a bad crowd...not even with the crowd of negative voices that sometimes take up residence inside your head.

Cheerleaders realize they are still on display, even when they are not wearing the uniform. Cheerleaders have a structure in their life. They have high morals they hold themselves to. They are usually healthy and keep themselves attractive.

Once a Cheerleader, Always a Cheerleader

One of the girls I most admired in Junior High was a cheerleader - a gorgeous, poised brunette, the class president and an excellent public speaker. When we got to Senior High, I tried out for the squad and made varsity cheerleading. Debbie did not.

Debbie held no grudge as we walked back to the bus. She said she was glad I had made cheerleading. Debbie was still a cheerleader in my book. She had just cheered for me, and that was what cheerleading was all about.

The "Outer" Inner Cheerleader

In our lives and businesses we are all on that field playing, but unlike cheerleaders, business owners have different standards. While cheerleaders usually subscribe to a given value set, you do not know the particular path each business owner took to get where she or he is. You do not know what someone's values are just because they own a restaurant, a print shop, or an international corporation. They could be someone you can trust or maybe not. But you usually know what a cheerleader's values are. It comes with the territory.

In business, your every action displays who you are to the world. As a result, most athletes that go into business usually make good business owners.

Those athletic business owners know that at first it takes a lot to make a little. Then the business can grow a lot. They know you have to give before you receive. Cheerleaders are athletes. Like a successful athlete, your values will determine the breadth, width and scope of your success.

IF YOUR VALUES ARE GREAT....
PEOPLE WILL RELATE

Real Value

In the first book of cheers, called *Just Yells*, Willis Bugbee said in 1927, "The cheerleader where once was merely tolerated is now a person of real estate." Wow. You can be a person of real estate. That means you have tangible value! Let the cheerleader inside you bring that value out because the only true real estate you ever own is inside your skin.

Now what can YOU do
to pump yourself up before your BIG game?

Chapter 3

BEFORE THE GAME

Confidence is being ready.
Stein Eriksen
Olympic Champion Skiing Legend

Failure to prepare is preparing to fail.
John R. Wooden
Head Basketball Coach, Emeritus, UCLA

www.yourinnercheerleader.com

BEFORE THE GAME

C heerleaders do general cheers before and between the games, but during the game they cheer for a specific action to take place. Not to win the whole game, but a "GET A FIRST DOWN" cheer, a "DE-FENSE" cheer or a "GET THAT BALL" cheer. Specific and focused cheers when playing: general cheers when preparing and pumping up. Let's get energized first, before we play.

1.   BEFORE THE GAME, PRACTICE YOUR ROUTINES

When nothing seems to help,
I go look at a stonecutter hammering away
at his rock perhaps a hundred times without as
much as a crack showing in it.
Yet at the hundred and first blow it will split in two,
and I know it was not that blow that did it,
but all that had gone before.
Jacob Riis

Prepare for the situations where everything counts and is on the line well before you're in those situations, at a time when it *does not* count. Find the things that work for you. Role-play the scenarios so that you have your cheers so "set" in your mind that you can pull them up automatically under duress, or even when it is really exciting - when YOU start winning!

Practice your cheers until they become habits. If you are often around positive people, they cheer you up. Things seem a lot easier being with them. You focus on positive things when you are with them. You get a feel for it. Eventually, though, you will need to learn to do this for yourself. If you have been relying on others, there will come a time when life will give you the opportunity to do this for yourself, by removing the sources you relied on.

For, you see, you cannot use another's positive attitude to keep uplifting you. That is not good for either of you. Reliance on others means that you will not grow so that you can reach that positive state for yourself and do it on your own. Then YOU can be the inspirational source for others until they, too, can do it for themselves.

An actor knows his lines before he goes on stage or in front of the camera. Did you ever see someone who has not practiced before a performance? They do not show respect for themselves, their work, or others if they did not take the time to learn their lines. That is different from stage fright. Sometimes we get into tough situations. That is when it is especially important that we are able to go on autopilot. Practice pays off. It is like reciting a mantra or affirmation that becomes so ingrained we hardly have to think about it.

There has to be something you can tell yourself before those important calls, before those meetings, that will support you to win, to have courage. "YOU CAN DO IT!" works. Use it. Simple. Clear. Effective.

The Lesson: Before the big game, have a
system in place for your success.

PRACTICE PRACTICE
ACT "AS IF"

LEARN IT AND YOU'LL EARN IT

2. GO TO TRAINING CAMP EVERY SUMMER

Sharpen the saw, polish the silver, and pump up the tires. At training camp, (e.g., business seminars, workshops and conferences), you will see the latest and greatest in your field. You meet others and they get to know about you. You will be inspired by those in the same boat, or by those in bigger and better models. You come back re-motivated! Use those seminars like a cheerleader uses training camp - to learn. Your business needs to get plugged in once in a while to a good learning source, a source of energy.

In addition to keeping up with the latest in your field, you will always have something that you need to know or to improve upon that can take you to the next level. Find a seminar that will fill those gaps for you. If you need to learn to network better, find a networking class. If you need to learn a computer skill, take a computer class. If you need to learn about investments because of all the money you are now making as a result of doing your inner cheers, take as many classes in investments as you can.

> *I was fortunate enough to learn the fundamentals*
> *at an early age from my teacher*
> *Jack Grout, and every year I would go back to*
> *Jack for my "annual checkup."*
> *Every year go back to your professional teacher*
> *and request a lesson about the basics.*
> Jack Nicklaus

When the Student is Ready, the Mail Appears

Whenever any financial seminar advertisement came to my home, I usually tossed it out; that is, until I needed to learn what to do with some money I had acquired. That provided the motivation. Then a brochure arrived from an investment company offering a seminar and dinner at a great restaurant. I thought, "Why not?" When I was at the seminar I sat next to a nice retired couple. The man had owned several very successful businesses, and we talked for quite a while. I asked them what would be the most important thing I could do for my financial future. The wife quickly answered, "Go to as many seminars like this as you can. Learn as much as you can." I have been doing that. When you start to learn, the Universe puts all kinds of opportunities in your face. That is no coincidence.

Training Camp Motivates

What is the difference between a speaker and a trainer?
The crowd is focused on the speaker to motivate them
but a trainer is focused on the crowd to motivate themselves.
T. Harv Eker

Go to training camp every year. The game is always changing and cheerleaders have to be at the very top of their game. They get ideas from other cheerleaders and trainers. They learn new cheers and get plenty of motivation. They get a chance to show their best stuff! The excitement they build during the summer carries over to the fall and winter - like storing nuts - little pockets of energy. So too, can you find the seeds that will grow your business at a training camp. Schedule at least one trade show, seminar or workshop to attend each year.

The Lesson: When it is your time to learn, embrace it.

GET TO CAMP
AND UP THE AMPS

3.   START EVERY GAME WITH A CLEAN SLATE

Each game goes back to 0-0. That is okay. Cheerleaders do not get discouraged. They always start with no score. Many of you have started a business with no numbers. You had to get some numbers. Those zeros are important, especially when they are strung together at the end of other numbers, like 5,000,000.

A football game starts at 0-0. The goal of the game is to get to the 0-yard line, the end zone. So the goal is to go from nothing to nothing, but take an exciting journey in between, like life. A full circle.

Things need to be set right before they can move forward. They need to be rebalanced. We slide into this life. We play around or fumble around and leave. But we can also touch people and make great inspiring plays while in the game. Each moment is a clean one.

Begin at the zero point. Each day life gives you a zero to zero score. What are you going to do with it? Do you have a daily goal for that score? HMMMM. Meditation is one way that takes you back to 0-0 on a daily basis.

A practical application of the zero point in your everyday life is when you forget something. Go back to the physical place and body position where you had your thought, and chances are high it will come back to you.

Every call, every proposal, every meeting is a fresh one. A new start, zero to zero. Treat it that way, and all your relationships, business ones included, will improve. Guaranteed. Your eyes will be fresh. Your mind will be fresh. It is clean. It's 0-0. It is nothing. And from nothing, *anything* is possible.

EVEN A HERO
STARTED WITH ZERO

4. MAKE SIGNS TO ENCOURAGE THE TEAM

Cheerleaders make signs to encourage the team and they put them up everywhere, especially on the day of the big game. I have signs on my computer, my refrigerator, medicine cabinet and under my clear desk pad. My friend Adrian wrote "signs" on our meeting agenda when I gave an important speech. He wrote, *"Be big. Be bold. Smile."* Little reminders, little "encouragers" that worked beautifully. Cheerleaders put signs everywhere to remind them of success. Do you do that before the big game?

I have two very important messages that I came across while reading (a very good source for finding signs). One is for my music, a quotation about the components involved in creating great music. The other message I keep in my office is a wonderful reminder to shape your work around one clear idea and let the audience discover their own interpretation and meaning from that one theme. You will find quotes that really touch your heart and when you do, pay attention.

Finding the quotations that resonate with you will help move your life forward. You will know a great quotation for you when you read it or hear it. It is like you are a guitar and someone has just strummed the perfect note on you. You will feel it reverberate very strongly in your entire being. That is the quotation for you. Use it to motivate you toward your success.

MAKE SOME SIGNS
SO THINGS ALIGN

While writing this book, I saw a big burgundy truck driving around. I call it the "Cheering Truck" because, as it passed me, in big bold letters all across the back door were the words BECAUSE I CAN AND I WILL. Now that's a big sign! Maybe someday you will see that red cheering truck. If you do, let me know where it is.

Put up motivating signs where you will see them and read them every day. I tape them on my bedroom door and see my signs several times a day.

SURROUND YOURSELF WITH SIGNS OF SUCCESS
THEN WHEN YOU ARE DOWN OR UNDER DURESS
YOU'LL FEEL MUCH BETTER I MUST CONFESS
AND THINK ABOUT YOUR PROBLEMS LESS

5.   HAVE AN EGG SALE

One little-known task of cheerleaders is to raise funds. Yes. Those peppy little things in short skirts are actually budding entrepreneurs.

In most businesses you will need to raise money. As cheerleaders, we had EGG SALES. We had to be innovative. In Wisconsin, if we scheduled a car wash, God usually scheduled rain.

How many of you have had an egg sale? It is a brilliant marketing concept. You go to one house, tell them you are trying to raise money and ask them if they have an egg. Who is going to refuse you an egg? Every good neighbor will lend an egg. Then, nothing out of your pocket, you go to the next house and sell them the egg. Nowadays, there may be some FDA regulations on this, but the concept is what matters. Find a way to get what you need. There will be a way. Wow! You can make a whole $16.58 in an afternoon! Market something more valuable than an egg, and who knows how much you can make?

Something as insignificant as an egg drove our whole fundraising campaign for two sets of uniforms, pompoms, wool jackets, shoes, and summer camp. Something in your business is like that egg. Find it and nurture the new growth.

You all have an egg.
Where is it?
Look...
It is right there, waiting for you to see it.

6.   COME UP WITH NEW ROUTINES

As cheerleaders we were always working on something new as well as practicing the beloved traditional cheers. We could really inspire an audience with a peppy, catchy, new cheer that made the crowd FEEL better. We were connecting people in a common cause.

Cheerleaders Know the Routine but They Do Not Get Bored

They know the score. The cheering routine is a pattern, but the energy put into that pattern is what ignites it, fires it up, makes it work. Cheerleaders put energy into routines.

Up-to-Date

Update your image, your product line, your materials, your thinking. Are you thinking the same thoughts of success that you did 6 months ago? Or are you thinking the thoughts you need to get you where you want to go tomorrow? Your thoughts and feelings point the way. Pick new routines to get new places.

TO GO NEW PLACES
CHOOSE THOUGHTS THAT ARE ACES

Are folks on to your old routine? Even if you have a favorite restaurant, you do not eat there every night. People love some tradition and something new, like the wedding rhyme for luck, "Something old, something new, something borrowed, something blue."

Whenever I would change the routine for my aerobics classes, the attendance immediately picked up at least 25-50%. Word got around I had a new routine. Everyone came to see what music I used, to see if they liked

36

it, and to see if they could do it. I used that new routine for a while. Then I'd have to develop another one. I was always creating something new to give the audience what they wanted. They rewarded me with attendance and enthusiasm.

Todd Canedy, one of the contributing authors of the best-selling book "Wake Up...Live the Life You Love," says most people believe that we hate change, but the fact is that we LOVE to change. We change cars, houses, jobs and clothing.

> *People actually like change.*
> *What they don't like is change without benefit.*
> Todd Canedy

Because cheers are fun and done in the special way that the brain likes to use for learning, they help us "change" our minds easier. Cheering is a strong, powerful, fun and effective way to change and direct our minds.

> *All good things continue only if they change.*
> John Harricharan

CHANGE FEELS STRANGE
At first...until you see the pay-off. Then it feels good!

> *When you're through changing, you're through.*
> Bruce Barton

7.   NEVER GET ON A BUS ALONE WITH THE WHOLE FOOTBALL TEAM

Football players are pretty wound up before a game. When our team had out-of-town games, the cheerleaders would go on the bus before the players to decorate it. Once I got caught on a bus as the team walked into it... the whole team, but no coach. I still remember some of the comments as I struggled to get back to the front of the bus. One of the players jumped onto one of the seats. In a hawking style voice he said, "She walks, she talks, she *crawls* on her belly like a reptile." Where did these guys learn this - the Barnum and Bailey Football Academy? While he was kind of cute, I was glad to get to the front of the bus.

Now I was never in danger, but I was in a perfect position to be teased. They took full advantage of it, as teenage boys will. However, in other circumstances, these football players would have given their lives to protect the cheerleaders. In fact, during one game, the fans of the opposing side started to criticize our cheerleaders. Boy, did that tick off our guys! They began to cheer back, "Our women cheer. Our women cheer!" We were only 17- and 18-year olds, but that chant made us feel very supported and proud of our school.

The Lesson: If you're going into an arena where you might be outnumbered, have some strong people on your side.

The Name of the Game

Are you little, like Little Red Riding Hood? Is it you vs. the wolf at the giant corporation? A strategy I learned when working with corporations is to get a name. A name gives you an entrance and someone on your side. Develop a relationship with the name first.

If at First You Don't Succeed...Get a Name
(i.e., a Sponsor) to Help You

I needed to get an Olympic license for some footage for one of my ski projects. The film was absolutely necessary to tell the story. The filmmaker who owned the rights to the footage gave me his permission. It was shot in 1952, before the Olympic Committee even knew they needed or could own these rights. The person in the films gave me permission too, but the USA Olympic Committee said I needed to get a license anyway. That is like Uncle Sam taxing the Indians for land they took away from them!

I called the Olympic Committee to tell them I had a very small budget for this project. They quoted me the same rate as NBC pays. Gulp. Yet I needed that license. I kept calling.

When you are doing your own project, it can take years if the funds are all your own. I did what I could do at the time and then had to let it go.

A year went by. I called the Committee again, told them what I needed, how the footage would be used, explained the scale, and got lucky. I guess because of the bustle of the upcoming Olympics, they had much bigger things on their minds. I explained that I intended to work with them again and wanted to develop a good relationship with them. I told them I needed to get a great rate to get this first of three ski projects off the ground. A new person was on the Olympic Committee then. She quoted a rate that was one third of what I was first quoted!

First, I developed a relationship. I made the Olympic Committee employee and myself into a team. Then the employee went into her own corporation to bat for me.

I did not walk on the bus alone this time.

The same thing happened with a license from NBC I needed for a *Tonight Show* segment. In fact, this was even a little more frustrating because Johnny Carson himself gave this footage to us. One spring day I was filming with Olympic skier Stein Eriksen. He played tennis with Johnny on his lunch break, then we resumed filming. (That is why Stein was an Olympic Champion. And he was 65 years old at the time!) Later that day, Stein showed me a hilarious videotape that Johnny Carson had given him at lunch. It was of Stein teaching Johnny how to ski on *The Tonight Show*.

NBC quoted me such an exorbitant rate that I could not use the film even though it was fantastic footage of Johnny Carson's first attempts at skiing. His expressions were priceless! Sometimes you just have to let it go when it does not seem to work despite all your efforts.

When the project was almost complete, Stein and his wife, Françoise, told me again that it sure would be great to have that *Tonight Show* footage because the segment was so funny. Well, I thought, "Why not try again and see what happens?" This time I was quoted a fraction of what they had said before. Months later, when I was actually having the license drawn up, there was a new person at NBC who was doing the paperwork. When she found out about my license rate, she was appalled. "I never let a license go for less than..." and she quoted a number with way too many zeros following it!

Now I could have gotten a little concerned except the film gods were favoring me on this one. *The Tonight Show* footage from the 1960s was inadvertently burned. A workman threw it in the incinerator in New York, thinking the boxes were marked "destroy."

Who held the Ace now? NBC desperately wanted to get a copy of my footage for their vastly shrunk archives, which I arranged to get to them. Sometimes the game is fun. Sometimes our feelings get injured in the game of life. But the game is always fascinating. The Big Game is always worth playing

If You are Going Into the Jungle of the Marketplace, You May Need Help Cutting Through the Branches

Let's say you are putting together a sponsorship package for your company. The package will be stronger when you already have a sponsor and include that in your proposal. That way, you go in strong, with a name. That is how the big deals are put together. However, make sure that a new sponsor is not in competition with the sponsor you have already secured. If

I had taken a competing team with me on that bus with the whole football team, there would have been a riot.

> FIND A NAME
> GET TO KNOW THE NAME
> THEN PLAY THE GAME

Everyone thinks corporations move very slowly, when in fact the opposite occurs. If you are trying to get money from them, they are ready to stampede you. You are in the bullring. The bull sees you and you are history, unless you get a BIG name. That name is like going into the ring behind the matador. He knows what to do to keep you safe. When you are behind the matador, the bull does not attack you. The matador knows how to handle him. Get a name.

> A NAME IS THE KEY
> TO THE DOOR OF THE COMPANY

Now I will share with you a little secret that many of you already know. Sometimes the best name you have to go in anywhere with is the name of the man upstairs. If you keep that name in your heart, the doors will open for you because the man upstairs knows everyone.

Your Name in Lights

Another way is to get a name...for yourself. Build a reputation in your field so that your name is the one that will open doors. "Hello, my name is Madonna." "Hello, my name is Cher." They get in. Perhaps you can get well known in your field. It will open doors for you.

Do you know the name Tiger Woods? My friend, Jack Nichols', son went to school with Tiger Woods when Tiger was in the 10th grade. The world did not yet know his name, but by the time Tiger was in 12th grade, there were scouts following his golf team around, and every one knew about the new sensation, Tiger Woods. His golfing teammates were kind of floored by his sudden notoriety, but do you think Tiger was suddenly getting doors opened for him? You bet!

GET A NAME

AND GET SOME FAME

8.   REMEMBER YOUR SCHOOL SONG

True joy comes as an expression of our inner music.
Greg Anderson

Your school song is your mission statement. Keep your mission statement in mind. If you don't have one, write one. Write your purpose in life and sing that "song" when you need to be motivated to win. Cheerleaders sing their school song with enthusiasm and passion. The song of your life will be in your mission statement. Sing it.

One of the beautiful songs the Kathi Burg Band sings is called *Good Enough for a Song*. In explaining the lyrics, Kathi says that we are *all* good enough - all worthy of a song. And that's really what a school song or mission statement is all about.

9.   SURROUND YOURSELF WITH OTHER CHEERLEADERS

And how impressive it is to see such a focused and positive team! When you surround yourself with highly positive people, you can achieve stunning results in life. If you surround yourself with "fear" leaders - who aren't true leaders by the way - even if you yell VERY LOUD and exert every ounce of your energy, those "fear" leaders will drown out your wonderful cheers with their whines, blames, warnings and complaints. As you say *I CAN DO IT!* you get barraged with *Says who? That's dangerous, YOU?,* and way too many other "fear" cheers to list here.

Fear can be very creative. It can sneak up and attack before you know it. If you surround yourself with cheerleaders, fear has a much, much tougher time finding and getting through to you. Do not take any "fear" leaders with you into the game unless you are willing to accept defeat. I don't know about you, but the thought of playing with people unraveling my cheers as I do them is not how I want to spend my life. It's more fun when we all cheer one another along from a place of love.

Get some great teammates. Choose "touchdown" people for your life. People that will run with you or protect you as you run toward your goal. Teammates who will cheer for you when you win.

I had only one choice about the company I kept.
It would only be with people who brought out the best in me.
Queen Latifah

10.   ALWAYS BE WILLING TO PROMOTE YOUR TEAM

A man's most valuable capital is the men he picks out to work with him.
James Buchanan Duke

You cannot predict whether someone will be loyal. That is a risk you take. But YOU can be loyal, and that is a trait worth developing. The people who help you deserve your support. Be loyal. By promoting others, they can succeed faster. The whole world gets better.

Cheerleaders are good at Public Relations. They are walking advertisements for the team they represent. They are always promoting someone or something.

"Dave, Dave, he's our man. If he can't do it...no one can."
Sure pumps up Dave's ego. How could it hurt yours?

Promote your work, your passion, with a passion.

Promoting Movie Ingenuity

After the Columbine shooting, my friends Chet Thomas and Darren Fletcher decided to take positive action and do something immediately to help at-risk youth. They used this event, tragic as it was, to challenge the movie industry to do something to positively change our world. They offered a summer class to teach inner-city kids the movie business. Through their contacts they got their industry peers to donate their time and make a 35mm feature film, teaching the kids how to make a movie in the process. The films were stunning because they were made by the same people who make Jerry Molen's films. Chet works for Jerry, who did a few little pictures like *Jurassic Park* and *Minority Report*.

When Chet asked me to do the PR for this event, I said, "Yes. I would be happy to." Because it was a great story, I was able to get it in *The Hollywood Reporter*. When the writer came out to collect information and take pictures, he loved what he saw and told Darren that we made the front cover. This is a HUGE accomplishment in Hollywood.

Ironically, another tragic event prevented that cover from taking place. We were scheduled for September 21, 2001. The horrible events of the attack on the World Trade Center occurred ten days earlier. The story still ran in *The Hollywood Reporter*. We got the middle page instead, which is a great spot. But we had come close to getting a front-page story in the largest trade journal in the movie industry.

Chet knows we almost had it once. And maybe Chet's boss, Jerry Molen, knows it too. And maybe, just maybe, there is the tiniest possibility that Jerry Molen's partner, a chap by the name of Spielberg, heard about it as well.

That is the power of PR. It grows and travels and you don't know where the winds that carry ideas and news will take it. The *winds of success* just might carry it to the right person.

It used to be that being on *The Tonight Show* would make or break your success. Now getting on *Oprah* during the afternoon is what sets many careers in motion. Who will be the next Oprah and what will that person be like? Here is a great PR opportunity.

Loyalty
"GO TEAM GO!"

Cheerleaders represent the team and do cheers mainly for teamwork. Sometimes you support the individual because it helps the team. Maybe you need to support one of your team members to break through a barrier, which can help everyone on the team. This can take some time, but if the whole team benefits it will be worth taking that time. If the team is focusing on its goals, helping a team member reach a new level can be a profound thing to witness. Be true to your team. Loyalty earns you trust and respect.

> BE TRUE TO YOUR TEAM
> AND YOU CAN REACH YOUR DREAMS
> and often far more...

11.   HOLD A PEP RALLY - IT'S GREAT PR!

How do cheerleaders build excitement for the upcoming game? They have a pep rally. Pep rallies get people excited to attend your event.

What if Christmas came all of a sudden with no preparation? Preparation is part of the fun! Start cheering early. For marketing big events, the major players send out several pre-event messages, encouraging you, "cheering you" to attend, where you will hopefully be motivated even more. They send emails, postcards, they phone. They keep cheering for their event.

There is a freeway direction on-ramp sign in Orange County, California, at Harbor Boulevard and the 405 Freeway. It is clearly marked and positioned well in advance so it allows you plenty of time to get into the correct lane and merge onto the freeway smoothly. Many of the on-ramps in Los Angeles are very difficult to figure out because the signs for them are so close to the on-ramp entrance that you usually see them after you no longer have a chance to get into the correct lane. Only by sheer guessing are you in the lane where you are supposed to be to get on the freeway.

Pep rallies are reminders of the game well in advance - to prepare you. They bring people together and motivate them. Do you motivate your customers BEFORE the sale? Give your customers a great pep talk and serve them through your own pep rallies. A pep rally helps keep the game in mind.

GET SOME PEP
IT'S A GREAT FIRST STEP

Before the game of life, every day, I do five to ten minutes of real cheers to get me motivated to succeed that day. I choose cheers to work toward the goals in life I am aiming for that day. I feel GREAT doing these cheers, and it gets me into a wonderful state of mind. I hold a daily pep rally!

A GOOD PEP RALLY
MAKES A BETTER FINALE

With this preparation as a base, you are now ready to play. It's a big beautiful game all around you just waiting for you to get in there and play it and win.

Now it is time.

Let's take your Inner Cheerleader to...**The Game**.

www.yourinnercheerleader.com

Chapter 4

DURING THE GAME

Life is about placing yourself in a position to win.

Jack Nicklaus

www.yourinnercheerleader.com

DURING THE GAME

D uring the game all your skills, values, practice and understanding come into play. This is when you are under pressure, working with others, and playing within a certain set of rules. It is when part of you goes on automatic pilot, but you want to make sure the pilot knows how to fly the plane! Though cheerleaders have prepared, there are still elements to remember during the game. Here is what cheerleaders do during the game to ensure they contribute to the success of the team.

1.   START THE GAME WITH A BIG KICK-OFF

The bigger you make your kick-off, the closer you are to your goal. So make it great. What can you do to ensure the biggest possible kick-off when you begin something?

2.   GIVE IT AS MUCH ENERGY AS YOU'VE GOT

A man can succeed at almost anything for
which he has unlimited enthusiasm.
Charles Schwab

This is your performance, your presentation, your dream off the shelf and into the market. Your dream is in the world's stadium. Cheer loud enough so that the deepest part of you hears. You do not have to use a megaphone, but you do have to get your message across. If you put out lots of energy ...*it will come back.*

You will need high energy to succeed. My mentor talked to me first about my energy, how I eat, what I eat, and when I exercise, before he ever mentioned film work. A good director cannot run out of energy and must know how to take care of herself.

51

The energy you put into your dreams is a special kind of energy. It goes out into the world in ways you cannot imagine. It touches people and comes back. It changes the world and it changes you.

Nothing great was ever achieved without enthusiasm.
Ralph Waldo Emerson

The Lesson: Make Your Point with Enthusiasm!

Enthusiasm means *God within*. Ted Corcoran, former International President of Toastmasters, says, "It is a fire, a flame, a passion within you."

Real enthusiasm is not something you have one day and not the next. Rather it is something you have all the time," According to Deepak Chopra, enthusiasm even reverses aging!

Be sincere. Use passion. Be an exclamation point in people's lives!!! Not a question mark or a comma.

COME ALIVE
BE STRONG
CHEER, CHEER
CHEER YOUR LIFE ALONG

3.   BUILD LOTS OF POSITIVE ENERGY

A positive person is someone who's hugging the moment.
Norman Lear

How many of you have ever sent a letter of complaint? I certainly have. Those letters are important if something needs to be addressed. Now how many of you have ever sent a letter of praise to a business? Yes, I've sent those too. How many of you send more letters of complaint than praise? The letters of praise stand out to a company. If you're a business owner, do you put letters of complaint on your office wall? I don't. But I have some special letters of praise that keep me motivated when I need them.

I have a brilliant friend, Jim, who was the sound engineer on my first two music recordings. He went on to engineer for a then unknown group that was always practicing in his studio. Their name... *No Doubt.* They made a little album called "*Tragic Kingdom*" which earned him seven platinum records.

Jim moved to Florida and took a job he loved in sound engineering. He framed those platinum records and put them on his living room wall. Then he lost his job after he had just bought a new house. At a time like that you could really get discouraged and, believe me, Jim did. But he looked at those platinum records shining on his wall and realized that he had done some good things. I think he has done some great things because those are not the only platinum records on his wall. By focusing on some of his big accomplishments, he was able to get out of the slump and get an even better job.

Put your most positive energy around you. Wrap it around you. Wear it. Revel in it. Soak it up. Put your energy into signs. Keep a few of them nearby for when you need them.

Are you spreading cheer or are you spreading fear?

4.   STAY IN SYNCH WITH YOUR TEAM

One of the things that we've learned in the field of personal change is that a nurturing support team is almost essential, particularly if you seek change that is real and sustainable.
A. Roger Merrill

The Deer Valley Resort DV8s, a precision ski team, are an amazing group to watch perform. They ski in synchronized formation. They do their routines on the mountain dressed in striking yellow outfits. The Thunderbirds, the Air Force pilots, fly incredible patterns in the air. They command attention in the sky. The Tommy Bartlett Water Ski Show in Wisconsin Dells features water skiers who perform synchronized stunts on the Wisconsin River. *A Chorus Line* is entertainment and perfection on stage.

Where can YOU present a unified front?

Henry Margenau, a physicist, used the Greek word *onta* (being) to describe individual elements that merge with one another to become something much more than the sum of the two. I think he was "onta" something. Forgive me.

1+1=eleven.

Mark Victor Hansen

If you work with a team - and all successful people do - stay in tune with them. Present a unified front when you are on display. See each team member as part of a unified whole but making different contributions. Work out the kinks, ideas and differences in your practice sessions. Give your best and blend with your team...when the clock is ticking. The power of the group exceeds and expands anything you can do on your own.

When you go out and perform in unison, something powerful happens...something majestic. Your Inner Cheerleader needs to coordinate with your other selves. She needs to cheer for your business self, your relationship self, your passionate self. When your inner selves are in unison and in harmony, you are a force to reckon with.

The Limelight

What if a cheerleader took the spotlight and hogged all the attention for herself? She would not be part of that squad very long. Cheerleaders do not showboat. They merge their strong outgoing personalities with other strong personalities to create an even more powerful force.

Like drops of water blend to form great waves, so enthusiasm blends to create a great group of cheerleaders. Cheerleaders are a supportive and motivational system for the crowd and the team. Sometimes you are a cheerleader for your game. Sometimes you cheer for another's game. It is all about the result.

Cheerleaders get in synch with other people. They get noticed. People like things that look organized. Cheerleaders look organized when they go out on the field and wear the same outfits to help stay in synch.

Things that are in groups are pleasing to the eye. A flock of birds is stunning. A field of flowers is beautiful. Twins are adorable, especially when they are dressed alike. In my hometown we had a set of triplets. This was a little town of 10,000 people. Everywhere these girls went they got noticed.

What can you do to make sure your team is in synch and on time? How can you get a great rhythm to your routines? What can you do to enhance the synchronicity of your team? Act in unison and know what the person in the front line is doing.

Master the Mind with Others

You may have heard of a mastermind group. This is a group of successful individuals who get together to become even more successful by sharing ideas and connections.

I joined a group of entrepreneurs who met every Wednesday. We focused attention on several of the members each night. That member would give the group their goal, problem or challenge. We would just pour our energy and ideas into them. It was such a kick to see their dreams get off the ground, or to see them overcome a business obstacle. The result of having that many focused individuals helping each other was profound. We were in synch with each other's dreams. Dreams manifest easier that way.

Be in synch with others, and together you are a strong, strong force. Four wheels rolling in different directions cannot take you anywhere, but four wheels together with a car on top can get you all over the continent.

The Lesson: Remember.
It's about the game,
not the cheerleader.

GET IN SYNCH
FOR A SUCCESSFUL LINK

4. USE SHORT CHEERS WHEN THE GAME IS MOVING FAST

Keep It Brief

Cheerleaders know things can change fast out there on the field. They do not want to be doing one of their special showy cheers when everyone is glued to the action on the field. When the game is moving fast, they do short cheers like: "We want a touchdown, touchdown. Get a touchdown." Those short cheers really build the pressure, adding to the excitement on the field. Which is exactly what you want to do at that moment in the game.

Focus the Crowd's Energy on the Field

You are competing with a lot of action out there. The crowd is with the energy. If the energy is on the field – and it should be – direct the crowd's attention to the field, not to you.

Heat Up Your Goals

WHEN THEY TURN UP THE HEAT
KEEP IT SHORT AND SWEET

When the heat is on, it makes for a good game. If you take some olive oil out of the refrigerator, it takes a little while to uncoagulate. But if you apply some heat, like running it under hot water, it is usable almost immediately. Apply some heat to your goals. You will get there faster. Heat speeds things up.

Popcorn takes a while to heat up. You hear a pop or two. All of a sudden it starts to pop like crazy. Cheers add heat. When you change your core beliefs, you add the "heat" of a new belief. You might not "hear" anything for awhile, but then you start to notice a thing or two happening. This is good! If you keep the "heat" on by cheering, things really start to pop. Pretty soon your bag will be full and ready to enjoy.

If the game is fast, respond with the appropriate pace. Decide and act quickly to fit in with the pattern of the game at that point. Later you can take your time, but when the heat is on, beat it.

If things are moving really fast, decisions need to be quick. A director on a movie set makes hundreds of decisions in the average 16- to 20-hour movie day. You do not have time to get stuck on an issue. It ties everything up. If you are on the track for success, and many of you are, get into this habit now. Then, when your success comes, it will feel natural.

And it will be necessary to continue this even after you become successful, or the success will not last.

Here is an example of a concise work statement that includes acknowledgment (a cheer) and keeps the action moving: "Sue, that is a great point. Why don't you check with Dan first? See if there are any other considerations and get back with me tomorrow by 11:00 am."

SHORTEN YOUR CALLS WHEN BUSINESS IS BUSY
KEEP THINGS BRIEF SO YOU WON'T GET DIZZY

Too Fast to Be a Chicken

In my bigger, better decisions I acted fast, before I could chicken out. I knew Irvin Kershner was going to be at an event I attended. You may recognize him as the director of one of the best-loved films of all time, *Star Wars: The Empire Strikes Back*. I wanted to meet him if at all possible. I loved his work and deeply admired his success in my chosen field.

At the event I saw a very tall gentleman come in and heard someone greet him as "Irvin." Aha. There he was. Standing twenty feet away from me. Standing all alone. Here was my chance. I knew I needed to act quickly. It felt as though I was being pushed toward him to introduce myself. I had one tiny moment, a little golden opportunity to meet him.

I went over and introduced myself, telling him how much I admired his work. He listened and we talked for a while. Luckily, I had listened to that urging and was able to talk to one of my biggest film heroes. Irvin has since become my mentor and given me so much invaluable advice and help.

All from my accepting that little push to meet the big man.

The Lesson: The fastest bird often gets the worm

6.   ASSUME THE CROWD IS ON YOUR SIDE

This makes a big difference in impact because cheerleaders are not always worried about pleasing people. They just cheer with the appropriate cheer at the appropriate time. Their job is to cheer, not to worry. We do not want "worry" leaders. Just do your work and assume the crowd is on your side.

It's really quite simple.
When you speak to the positive in someone,
that energy begins to awaken in them.
Judith Orliff. M.D.

Before I had to give an important speech, I confessed to my friend Fawn that I hoped there would be some smiling faces out there in the audience. She told me. "Don't worry. They will all be smiling faces." That is one of the many reasons why Fawn is my friend. If you are going to assume anything, why not assume the positive, like Fawn did? Guess what? There were many smiling faces in that audience. But more important, I was smiling.

7.   KNOW YOUR GAME ...
And Know What Part of the Game You Are In

Everyone has seen a game where some cheerleader does a big happy cheer – when the other team has just scored. OOPS. Cheer for your good side, not your *other* side. Don't do "fear cheers." Cheer for your successes. Know what those successes are. Know what your successes will "look like." Know the essence of what you want. Have your goals so clear and focused like a laser, that you absolutely know when success knocks at your door. If you are expecting it, success is more likely to show up. Will it be a phone call that opens a big door for you? Go through it. Will it be an opportunity to say *Yes*? Jump on it.

Perfect Timing

Say *Yes* to opportunities even if you are not entirely prepared. When Conrad Hilton opened a new hotel, often many last-minute things still needed to be done. He said that there just comes a point when you have to say, that's enough and just open the doors.

Do you think you are too busy to say *Yes* to the opportunities in your life? Those opportunities will move on to someone else if you say *No*. Did you ever do something that you did not want to do but later something great came out of it? I was called one day and asked if I could fill in and give a speech at the very last minute, that same evening. I was not ready but I decided to challenge myself and give that speech anyway. I made the decision to do the best I could with the time I had. With just a tiny bit of preparation, I gave a speech done in an English accent about two old, charming English gentlemen. It was an absolute hit. Not only did I feel great afterward, but I would have denied the audience the entertainment from hearing that speech if I had said *No*.

What Part of the Game Are You in?

If you do not know the game has nine innings or that it takes one hour, you might use the wrong cheer or you might not pace yourself, leaving yourself out of energy just when you really need to push for success.

If you do not know that it takes eight calls on average before you will get an order, you might get discouraged by the second call. Find out the batting averages for your business and your field. Look in trade journals or on the Internet for these statistics.

By the way, it is no mistake that in business you are asked "What field are you in?" What is YOUR playing field? What are the rules of YOUR game? You can bet your best competitors know this.

KNOW YOUR GAME

TO GET THE FAME

8. KEEP GOING, DON'T DROP THE BALL

There are plenty of times in business when the energy is similar to a football game. If you have the ball, you are getting results and the openings are there for you – don't stop and wait for a better time. You'll get creamed. When you make a phone call, a sale etc., keep going. If that call leads you to another call, keep going. Keep the momentum up.

I made a series of calls one day on a big project. Every person I called was positive and led me to another person until I got to the ONE THAT REALLY MATTERED – the decision-maker. And then I waited for over a month to call him back. This was a mistake. I had the energy and momentum with me.

I justified doing this because I needed to have a new contract signed and it took that long. The day I mailed out the signed contract I called him back, but then I had to rebuild all that positive energy. I would have saved myself so much effort if I had called him right away when everyone was initially excited by it. In other words, I dropped the ball.

When you see an opportunity for success, take it and let it be known. The football player who catches a pass, runs with it. When someone throws a part of your dream to you, run with it – or you will get tackled and go nowhere.

9. CELEBRATE EVERY ACCOMPLISHMENT

The more you praise and celebrate your life,
the more in life there is to celebrate.
Oprah Winfrey

Life is a celebration. Do you celebrate your successes? Do you make it party time? What if you have just "failed"? Sometimes failure is a step toward success. Celebrate that you get to play! You are in the game! That alone is a huge accomplishment. You cheer for a child who is learning to walk or to ride a bike, even though they don't do it perfectly, even though they fall frequently. You know they are eventually going to walk, or ride that bike. You know sooner or later they will learn, even though they have never done it before.

In your business there will be some things you have never done before. You may fall a bit. But like that child, know that you will get there. Failing is part of success. You win by playing the game.

TO FAIL IS NOT TO LOSE
IF THE LESSON IS ONE YOU WILL USE

Here Comes the Sun...Finally

In Norway there is a deep valley, surrounded by the towering mountains the country is famous for, including the highest mountain in the land. The area is called Rjukan. Norwegians do not see the sun in this valley from October to sometime in February because the mountains are too high and Norway is so far north. When the sun finally returns to the valley skies, the people have a celebration. Something about Rjukan touched a deep chord within me. Being from California I thought, "How can they live without the sun for so long?" No wonder they celebrate!

Upon my return from Norway, I wrote a song about this intriguing valley, a love song from the Earth itself, yearning for the kiss of the sun. Celebrating life. Here are the first few verses for you.

LOVE SONG TO THE SUN

How I long for the mountains
How I long for the days
How I long for the sun
When the sun goes away.

Oh where do you fly to?
Oh why can't you stay?
'Cause the moment you left me
The warmth went away.

CHORUS
Give me the light that lights a thousand mountains
Oh please bring back the waterfalls and fountains
Give me a glow that last for a hundred days
Until I see your golden face again.

How I long to walk with you
How I need you by my side
Come back, surround me
And bring me alive

© 2005 White Wing Entertainment

The Norwegians know how to celebrate the cycles and victories of life. They know about belief and about holding on through the darkness. When given a chance to celebrate, they take it. Now the Norwegians know the sun will eventually return as it has done this many times before. Unlike the child who has never ridden a bike, the Norwegians are not really worried – just anxious and eager.

Whether a success is assured or doubtful, when the desired outcome arrives, it is a success! Celebrate! Every victory is to be celebrated. Do that for yourself. Believe in yourself, even when it gets dark and it seems as though the sun will never return to your life. It will. Celebrate like crazy when it does. And remember the little town of Rjukan, if you ever forget.

Another Norwegian, my friend Stein Eriksen, celebrates with a toast his mother taught him. He raises his glass in a toast to the joy he feels for the great ski life he is blessed with, "Na har vit det got igjen!" *We have it good again!* And the toast helps make it so. Celebrate every day.

10. READ THE FANS

Change tactics based on the crowd's response. Cheerleaders read the fans and then they change cheers. They read and they change. Cheerleaders know they do not need 100% cooperation from their audience, but they do need a majority. Your responsiveness is critical to your fans.

Cheerleaders can tell when the crowd needs waking up. SO WAKE THEM UP! How did Prince Charming wake up Sleeping Beauty? With a kiss. Kiss your dream awake. It is called love. Love wakes things up in your life. Use that power of love in your cheers and your game.

Do your customers need waking up? Do your clients have your "number"? If they were on a quiz show and were asked the following question, could they answer it?

"When (*your company*) calls, what is the first thing (*your company*) will say?"

Would they know the answer?

Avoid having them know you THAT well. Surprise them. Delight them. Wake them up to other possibilities - possibilities that only you can give them. You want them to be excited to talk to you because they NEVER know what you might have up your sleeve. Do you always keep it interesting? Do you keep them motivated? Working the crowd means finding out what they want and what they will pay attention to. Keep statistics. Try different approaches. Some will work, some won't. Do more of what works and you will be a success. This is Marketing 101.

The Lesson: Respond to the response.

NARRATE, TRANSLATE
BUT FOR GOODNESS SAKE ...COMMUNICATE!

11. GET THE MESSAGE ACROSS QUICKLY

DO IT WITH SIZZLE, DO IT QUICK
SO THE MESSAGE YOU GIVE WILL STICK

Quick.	Get the message there fast. Like email, make the communication instant.
Sizzle	Better have some fire or you can't cook up any business.
Stick	Let your message explode with impact. Blow away all your audience's doubts so your message will stick with them.

Business Example – USE A STRONG HEADLINE

Hi! Want $500 free?

OR

EVERYONE WHO SIGNS UP FOR THIS SEMINAR WILL GET $500!

Are you going to get takers? SURE! Putting together an ad with a description like the following will motivate and pique curiosity.

We are giving away a $500 value at this seminar. You will take away information that will save you at least $500 in taxes (or something of value to them). *Not only will you get that great information, but we are holding a drawing and one lucky person will take away **$500 in cash**!*

You get the idea.

I had a meeting with Arthur Lloyd, the former head of Amtrak for the West Coast. He had the power to give me unlimited train travel for my film crew, which was critical to expanding my program, *The Great Body Escape*. I flew up to San Francisco for our meeting. I knew what I needed from Mr. Lloyd. The first question he asked me, was, "What do you need from us?" I delivered my request and Arthur said, "Yes." He explained a few logistics and the meeting was over. In less than 10 minutes (minus air travel, of course), I had met my goal. Meetings don't have to be long. But they have to be clear.

The Lesson: Get the message across quickly.
It may be the only chance you have.

12.   CHEERLEADERS DON'T STAND IN FRONT OF A CROWD and think.   THEY YELL

If the message is worth saying...say it out loud.

YELL, YELL, YELL
WHAT YOU WANT TO TELL

Thinking is not doing. You have got to say it. And people need to hear it. Get the message out of your mind and into the world.

Air traffic controllers THINK, which is a very good thing too! It would be quite unnerving to see *them* yelling. Unfortunately some bosses have it backwards. They *think* their job is to yell. How many of your bosses yell positive cheers? Did you ever hear your boss coming down the hall, yelling: ***WAY TO GO, DALE! WHAT A GREAT SALE!***

Salespeople know they have to do this. So they hold sales rallies, which are beefed up pep rallies with prizes.

Words are powerful. Yelling them is even more powerful. A group yelling them is profoundly powerful.

What if cheerleaders just *thought* cheers to the crowd? It would be kind of weird. Watching someone thinking certainly is not motivational to me.

The Lesson: Unless you are at a
mind-reading convention, speak.

Cheerleaders give a whole new meaning to "Word of Mouth."

> *Knock Knock...*
>
> *Who's there?*
>
> *Ice Cream*
>
> *Ice Cream who?*
>
> *Ice Cream because I'm a Cheerleader!*

YOU DON'T HAVE TO PREACH, IF YOU'RE GOING TO TEACH
BUT IF YOU PLAN TO SELL, YOU'VE GOT TO TELL

13. KEEP CHEERING, EVEN WHEN YOU'RE NOT AHEAD

There are plenty of times you will not be ahead in a really good game. You do want a great game, don't you? At a critical point, if it appears you're losing, do not sit and quit. Cheer harder. Then cheer *even* harder. That is where success lives.

Did it ever appear that someone else was winning? Maybe sometimes you thought they did not deserve to win. Do you think life is unfair? Or do you think *high thoughts* – that you will get to your success eventually? That you will get your chance? That is how the Inner Cheerleader thinks.

And will you succeed?

Yes indeed! Yes indeed!

Ninety-eight and three-quarters percent guaranteed.

Dr. Seuss

Do Your Best and Forget the Rest

When a company I had been doing business with for several years called me and said out of the blue, "We're sorry, but we can no longer support your project. We are going to cancel our involvement," I had to think fast. I had to absolutely refuse to believe in anything but my dream. They were not just pulling the rug, but the entire floor, out from under my feet.

A few weeks earlier I had met with them and had received a positive response about this project. They requested a few changes in just a couple of areas regarding a safety issue. I made those changes and found some ways to improve the project even more. I bought myself some time after this surprising phone call by the response I gave them: "Just wait until you get the video from me. I sent you a copy by priority mail. You should have it tomorrow. Check it for the changes, which I think you will like, and call me back."

They did like it and everything was fine. If I had overreacted, I could have blown it all out of proportion, made them the bad guys and lost years of work. I had done my absolute best on the project. Now I had to sit back and let it go.

I think it was one of those big tests you get when you are *almost* there. Yes, I was scared and concerned, but I had to really cheer for my dream internally now. And just wait. It was like having a huge tornado roar through town. During that tornado, I had to just go in the basement and wait it out, hoping that something would still be standing when it was all over. I simply refused to believe that my project was dead. And somehow it survived. I did not give up, and neither should you when you are so close. A cheerleader does not go on the sidelines and sulk when the other team gets ahead. She takes immediate action and does her best cheering.

Those are the most important times to cheer for yourself, when it appears as though you face your biggest obstacle. But here is also where the biggest changes in your life result. As I said before, that is where success lives. You just have to do your best.

Don't look back. Leave it all on the track
From the movie *Racing Stripes*

Use "Right Thinking" to Get Ahead

I had been working to get funding for a video with Stein Eriksen, the Olympic ski champion from Norway. A man called and said he was from the MPCA. I had no idea what the MPCA was. He asked about my project with Stein: where I got the funding for it, who wrote the narration, etc. He asked lots of production questions and said that my work must have been a *labor of love*. Yes it was! Then he said that he had acquired the funding for doing a skiing video with Stein himself.

My first thought quickly darted toward disappointment, because I had wanted to do the project and get it funded myself. At this point I did not think I was ahead. I felt hugely behind in the game. I did not even feel like I was playing. Luckily, I pushed that disappointing thought out of my mind. Instead I chose this thought: "Stein deserves this." My response to this man was: "That's great. How can I help?" It was one of my better moments.

Because of my response, he invited me up to LA. It was there, at the Motion Picture Corporation of America, that I was asked to produce the project. All from a thought!

Reach, then reach again, like climbing a rope. That is how you get to the top.

Keep cheering and you will get ahead.

***The Lesson: The most critical time to cheer
is when you are not ahead.***

14.   DON'T TURN YOUR BACK ON THE FANS

Business is not like painting a picture.
You can't put a final brush stroke on it
and then hang it on the wall and admire it.
Ray Kroc

Your words ignite the passions of the spectators. The audience is who you are trying to motivate. Remember that. For in motivating others, you too will be motivated.

Face the Audience but Watch the Game

You do not have eyes on both sides of your head. But it would be great to see the future, the immediate moment and the past. The field is the potential. The audience is the present. Bring that potential to the present.

The spectators know the score. You know the score in your field, right? If you do not, how can you know what to cheer? Even if you know the score, you still have to fire up the crowd. Take note: the fans may be watching the game even if you are not. And if you have to turn your back on the fans, at least keep them in focus.

When the Team Needs the Cheer

Sometimes you need to let the fans be heard by the team, so all that good energy and encouragement gets through to the players. The team needs those cheers. A player knows that several hundred or thousand people on his side at a critical moment are motivating. The whole audience is on your side when you are cheering internally. You tap into a huge force.

In a real game the audience cannot be on the field, but they are with the players and the players know it. They feel the cheers. When you cheer for yourself, a deep part of you will hear and feel these inner cheers too.

When Your Customer Needs the Cheer

Customers are your audience. Your team is your business. If you have other things to do and to focus on at the moment, make sure you come back to your customers often, even just to smile and cheer them on. Give them some positive energy. Look at the game, get an update. Then let the fans know about it, even if they are looking at the same game and seeing the same thing you are. Show your customers you are with them, and your business will have the support it needs.

When You Need the Cheer

When you are going for a dream, do not turn your back on your goal. Keep it in focus. Keep cheering and motivating and looking your dreams right in the eye.

In Feng Shui, you never arrange furniture so that your back is to the door.

The Lesson: You can't back up to the present.

IF YOU SHOW YOUR BACK YOU RISK ATTACK
IF YOU SHOW YOUR FACE YOU WIN THE RACE

15. WHEN MOTIVATING OTHERS – ENCOURAGE, DON'T FORCE

GO TEAM GO!

Do not say it like you're whipping a horse. Instead, become one with that horse. That's when the horse responds. The horse and the rider working together.

Be ye not a lecturer but a guide. People would not go to games if it felt like school. Tour buses around London are packed, but Speaker's Corner in Hyde Park, London, where anyone can speak on anything, anytime, is much less crowded. Who wants to hear someone just voicing their opinion?

The strongest changes and most growth in my life have been the result of someone challenging me, not when someone tells me what to do. When you just do what you're told, you're like a sheep. But if you are the one responsible for the decision to take an action, then YOU have to change. You become the shepherd. A challenge expands you. A demand contracts you. There is a big difference in energy.

How to Motivate a Cheerleader

When we were holding auditions for Junior Varsity cheerleaders, we split into many groups to teach the aspiring cheerleaders the new cheers. I gave the group I was training a challenge to get their mind off their fear of learning the cheers. "Let's be the loudest group in here." The enthusiasm must have picked up 200%. Pretty soon every other group was kicking up the volume too. The room filled with energy. Every one had a much better time and learned the cheers faster by focusing on only one thing – volume. They had a specific and achievable goal.

73

16. BE A CHEERLEADER, NOT A FIREFIGHTER OR A FIRE EXTINGUISHER

Cheerleaders become the fire. Be the fuel of success. Get everyone fueled up, not burned out. Get *fired up*. Light the sparks that ignite the spirit of the audience.

Firefighter: "Oh no, their team got the ball! How awful! What a lousy call!"

Cheerleader: "We can get that ball again! Make that ball your new best friend!"

Nothing stops, nothing discourages a cheerleader. Not for long.

Cheerleaders create the messages that are necessary for a positive future. They do not focus on what they cannot control. Instead they focus on celebrations for successes recently accomplished and positive messages for the future.

Are Cheerleaders Defensive? NO!

Of course not! You do not hear cheerleaders scream, "Oh no! They got the ball! What are we going to do?" They see the ball was stolen, and they have an immediate and positive response: A turnaround cheer. "GET THAT BALL!"

Even giving up the ball is not necessarily bad. Cheerleaders know this. The defense can do as much damage on the field as the offense. For instance, they can get the offense reinstated at the 5-yard line and in a perfect position for a touchdown or goal. Sometimes in a game you have to ask, who did the job? Who won it — the offense or the defense? The defense can cause some positive things to happen on the field, like how many yards the opposing team had to give up. The defense can make the other team eat a ton of yardage.

Do Not Play the Defense. Play the Strategy

In conversation do you take the offense or the defense? If you start defensively, your partner may take the offense or vice versa. However if you refuse to do that and instead strategize together - you both win.

In the game of football, on the defense, anyone can hold the ball. On the offense, only certain players can. Only certain players in life will take the offense and run toward the goal. Are you willing to be one of them?

Anyone can become defensive. This prevents success. Few of us take the offensive, the ACTION to succeed. You cannot win without an offense.

Defense blocks. You have got to get through it. What is blocking your goals? Can you stop it? Do not BE offensive, but TAKE the offensive.

In companies, defense positions are often secretaries. These are sharp ladies, often sharper than their bosses. I worked with many of them. They are smart, funny and extremely capable. They know if someone is BS'ing them, and they respond to a warm, respectful tone in kind. Instead of trying to run over the defense, dance with them. By dancing, you still effectively continue moving toward your goal.

Do Cheerleaders Fall for a Fake Fire? NO!

Sometimes players fake injuries to throw off the other team. Someone will pretend to have a charley horse in his leg, and the opposite team notices it and leaves that side of the field unfortified - and they get clobbered. This goes on all the time. "Hey, look at that!" The *made ya look* syndrome.

Do not fight fires unless they are the real kind. The fire in your heart to succeed and to make a difference is the kind of fire you want. You wouldn't fight that fire, would you? Light that kind of fire in your work. Give it a flame that comes from your heart and soul.

How many of you are like an unlit candle, waiting for something to light your life? When are you going to start burning? Burning to find something you are so passionate about you *have* to do it? When are you going to start being a light for the world? Start using your energy for light.

IF YOUR DREAMS NEED SOME FIRE
YOU'LL FIND IT IN YOUR OWN DESIRE

The Lesson: You've got to stoke the fires
of your dreams or they go out.

17.   **REPEAT YOURSELF FOR EMPHASIS.**
       KEEP IT SIMPLE
       Repeat Yourself for Emphasis. Keep it Simple

Say it again and again if you have to. Until you get results. Get to the point. Do it again and remember that *again* is a "gain" - not a failure. Repetition and consistent action almost guarantee your success. Dreams should come with these instructions: ***Repeat to self as often as necessary.***

Simple Simon

FIRST AND TEN
DO IT AGAIN!

~ Or ~

"Let's cheer for that player over there, the one just getting up who ran ten yards from the 35-yard line to the 45-yard line before he got tackled. Let's see if we can all encourage him to go from the 45-yard line to the 55-yard line so we can get another first down."

Whew! The game might be over before you could say that! By then the crowd would be using this opportunity to buy popcorn, or worse, to throw it.

What does an umpire do?

"You're outta here." No details, just the facts.

When there is a group with a lot of energy saying the same, short, powerful message all together, we listen. Use that concept in your work.

The more you make things complicated,
the more there is to learn.
Keep things as simple as you can and
you have a chance to do them better.
I'd always rather do a few things well.
Coach John R. Wooden

Example

"Hello, Mr. Famous Person."

"Who is this?

"This is Terri Marie. How are you today?"

"What do you want? Do I know you? "

"No. I am a producer and I know you're really busy, but I am working on a project here and I would like to talk to you about it and see if you would be willing"...CLICK. "Hello, Hello???"

It does not work that way out there.

Busy, famous people, if you can get through to them at all, are like a fish that briefly jumps out of the water. You have a small opportunity to catch them and to reel them in. They do not want a polite "Here, little fishy." They want the "hook." Give it to them. Hit 'em between the eyes. Be strong first. Be nice too, but they need to see your strength, not your weakness.

Here's What Works

I attended an ASCAP (American Society of Composers, Authors and Publishers) meeting of 2,500 people. Unbeknownst to us, we had a special speaker that evening, Senator Orrin Hatch. Maybe you don't know that Senator Hatch writes music and is very involved in helping the music industry.

After the meeting, Senator Hatch quickly left down the center aisle. He is quite tall and was striding confidently with Secret Service men all around. I KNEW I had to talk to him about music for a project I was doing. He had a huge lead with those much-longer legs, but somehow, I managed to get in front of him. He and his men stopped. Facing them, I had one chance to say something.

These words popped out of my mouth: "Do you know Stein Eriksen?" He expected some music spiel. My question caught him completely off guard. It caught me off guard too! He said, "Yes, very well." "I am doing a project with Stein. Can I call your office?" I asked. "Yes," said Senator Hatch.

Because of that brief encounter, I now have two of his motivational songs on my latest project. Sometimes you just know a moment is for you.

The Lesson: Keep requests to others simple.

18. LET EACH TEAM MEMBER BE VIEWED TO THEIR BEST ADVANTAGE

It's hard for a fellow to keep a chip on his shoulder
if you allow him to take a bow.
Billy Rose

All people are important. One may shine at any particular moment, but all of them count. Ziegfield with his famous "Follies" had his dancers on a rotating stage so that the dancers in the back got the limelight for a while. As the stage turned, he brought everyone into that glowing light where the audience could focus on them. Even the dancers who were not stars were dressed in stunning costumes and beautiful hats and gowns. Everyone counted. Everyone was important.

Each Person is Unique

We had one cheerleader who could do a great back flip. When we were trying to show off a little bit, who do you think we put on display? We gave her the floor. We put the small girls in front or at the top. The short girls were better for some things, the tall girls for others. Success is using all of the best qualities of each person.

We had to take our squad, analyze the strengths and weaknesses of each cheerleader, and assign them positions. You already assign positions and priorities to things in your life. Do you put your goals where you can best see them and where others can best see them? Do you make it exciting to show others your goals - or are they buried under a huge player who is trying to block you?

SHOW YOUR BEST, FORGET THE REST

Have everyone put their best foot forward. Everyone has unique skills and talents. Use them. Each bud blossoms into a particular flower. With flowers it is easy to tell what each one is. With people it is not so easy to tell just by looking whether they are a gifted musician, mechanic, or doctor.

But that true essence of who they are will be evident when they have merged with their passion, because their inner quality attracts everyone. They are like perfect pitch. Clear and true.

When you are sure of your light, you do not mind letting others shine, even if your switch happens to be off at the moment. In fact, it makes your life and the whole world easier when others do shine.

Remember, if just one of 88 keys on a piano is missing, a song will not sound the same.

This happened to me in New York City. There in the lobby of the nice hotel I stayed at was a beautiful grand piano. The hotel clerk said they would love to hear some music when I asked if I could play. As I opened the shiny mahogany cover I noticed one key was missing its "ivory." That key happened to be one that I used in many pieces of my music. Playing around the missing high "G" was tricky. Some songs I could not play at all. That one little note was just too important. Yet when I could hit the high G it was magical. Every one of us has that magic place where we fit in perfectly. Look for that perfect note in all you meet.

The Lesson: There is a perfect place for everyone. Find yours.

EVERYONE IS SPECIAL
EVERYONE IS FINE
EVERYONE HAS A PURPOSE
LET EVERYONE SHINE

19. USE TIME-OUTS TO REMOTIVATE AND DO SOMETHING BIG

How much time do you allocate each week
to sitting back and reflecting
on what you do, why you do it,
and in which direction your life is heading?
David McNally

We saved some of our longer and better cheers for time-outs. We knew we had one minute to build more positive energy. During time-outs the crowd can't hear what the coaches are telling the players in the huddle because they are not in range. But the fans can focus more on the cheerleaders. The crowd's attention is not divided. Grab it.

Take time-outs. Breathe in. Do an inner cheer. It only takes a minute.

CHEERING A MINUTE OR LESS
CAN GET YOU MORE SUCCESS

Timing is Everything

In business, do not show your full package to clients right at the beginning, on the first call or the first meeting. Make a short presentation, and go back to your game. Wait until they decide to call you back into their game. This will be your "time-out." Then they will be more willing to listen to you and will give you more attention.

Create Time-Outs in Your Business

You would never see cheerleaders do all the cheers in the first quarter, then sit on the sidelines and drink soda for the rest of the game. Do not do all your cheers in the first quarter. Save some for time-outs and stretch them over the whole game. Like a timed-release Vitamin C, take time-outs during your day to do an inner cheer.

BEFORE SOMETHING BIG

DO AN INNER CHEER

YOU'LL HAVE A LOT *MORE* ENERGY

AND A LOT *LESS* FEAR

The Lesson: Take the time you need to motivate yourself to succeed.

Ready for a break? Every game needs a **half-time.**

TIME FOR A TIME-OUT

THAT'S WHAT THE NEXT CHAPTER IS ABOUT

Chapter 5

HALFTIME

Then we'd play some Broadway tune like the
theme from Oklahoma!
while forming what appeared to be a giant saucepan
but was meant to be the map of Oklahoma.
This is when most of the fans would either
go to the bathroom or yell,
"Why are you standing there forming a giant saucepan?
Bring back the dance squad."

...the rules for successful halftime entertainment were
set in my impressionable head for life.
Have a theme. Open with a big number.
Always have a dance squad.
Cut the bathroom break song.
End with a rousing fight song.

Don Hahn
Producer, The Lion King

www.yourinnercheerleader.com

HALFTIME

There are two sides to halftime. One is the side of the cheerleaders – the other is the side of the players. I'm going to give you both angles, because sometimes you will need to be the one encouraging and entertaining others and sometimes you will be in need of that motivation and/or relaxation. So this section is part performance and part R & R.

Halftime is the big entertainment section of the game for the cheerleaders, but it is a time for the team to rest and quickly analyze strategies and chart a better course if one is needed. When you're playing, take a break. When you're cheering, beef it up.

1.   HALFTIME IS A TIME TO REGROUP

Periods of recovery are...intrinsic to creativity
and to intimate connection.
It is in the spaces between work that love,
friendship, depth and dimension are nurtured.
Jim Loehr

There was a specific time that really stood out when I was a cheerleader. I had no energy that day. None. And we had a really big game later that evening. Throughout the school day I dragged myself through putting up the pre-game banners and the other tasks we had to do. Then I just sat in the bleachers wondering how I could possibly cheer through a whole game. While I was sitting there, I decided to go wash my face. I went into the lady's room and splashed cool, refreshing water on my face for several minutes. Somehow the water washed that dreary heaviness too. I came back cheery and energized. While it was just a little thing, it worked wonders. I had taken time to regroup.

You can regroup at set times or as the need arises. Set a benchmark goal. Get your team together to brainstorm. You may have to do things different in the second half of the game. If things have been going fine, do more of them. If they have not, change your strategy.

In business, pick a benchmark goal; let's say, after either two months or $150,000 in sales, whichever comes first. Then analyze and regroup. You do not fertilize the lawn only once. What can you do to WOW people after you have made your halftime goals?

What Works?

For a really big sale, how about sending a special gift? Send it unannounced three months after you made the sale, with a little note:
"Just to let you know that this is the 3-month anniversary of your first order. We'd like to let you know that we value the commitment on your part with this bouquet of roses." Or...

"Here is a blanket for the football game, along with tickets." Or...

"Enjoy these tickets to the baseball game. We love to go to bat for you."

Get specific. For smaller sales, like providing the cones in an ice cream shop, the important thing is to acknowledge the sale and the relationship, to remind the customer that you are interested and you want them to be happy with the sale.

Tip: I've found that regrouping works best AFTER you've done something to regroup from (i.e., AFTER the sale, not before). So in the space between their order and your follow-up, think about what you want to create with this customer and how you want to acknowledge them, before you take more action.

Personal contact is a great way to regroup. On large sales like a car or truck, a phone call 30 days after the sale to see if the customer is happy with the purchase works two ways. "I just want to make sure you are happy with item X." If they are not, you can correct it before too much damage is done. If they love the vehicle, they will love it even more when you call to verify their satisfaction.

A doctor in Southern California calls his patients a few days after their visit to see if they are feeling better and if their medication is working for them. Whether or not their body feels better, they certainly feel better about their doctor after this personal touch.

If you wish for a balanced life you must take the time to analyze things every so often. It will refresh you and give you a much clearer view. Wisdom comes from pulling yourself out of the game for a little while.

All significant, long-lasting, personal change
must usually begin in a quiet space that promotes
reflection which in turn leads to self-awareness.
You must withdraw from the hullabaloo of life
from time to time to give yourself an
opportunity to look within and explore
those areas that need transformation.
Herbert Benson, M.D.

Regroup at halftime. Measure your progress. Devise a new strategy if necessary.

2. HALFTIME IS A TIME TO SHOW YOUR BEST

There is no halftime in this business.
You don't even get to go to the locker room to rest.
Ross Perot

Perot could've been speaking about cheerleading. While we did get a small break, we savored halftime like a sportsman's dessert – for WE got the field – not the sidelines!

Cheerleaders shine during halftime. They do their wow 'em routines while the "players" are resting and regrouping. Halftime cheerleading routines have great music, more intricate high-energy moves – AND the best part – the fans are all theirs.

When you have no action on the field to distract you, you can give your full attention to something you plan and deliver spectacularly. Pick your best cheers and strategies. WOW 'em! Those who see halftime will appreciate the entertainment. True, some will go get food or leave the stands for a while, but when the players are resting, the spotlight is on you. You have the chance to deliver your BEST to the crowd. Use it.

This is like the opportunities in business when you have time to prepare a great proposal and then deliver it. Make it entertaining and perform it well. Do it in the time given to you, like a great halftime.

Now is the time to show your best stuff!

Lesson: When you are doing your commercial breaks, make sure they are entertaining.

3.   IF YOU WANT TO WOW THE CROWD, DO A FLIP

People love to be entertained, yes, but it involves a certain amount of risk to do something spectacular. Are you willing? What can you do in your work or in your life to be spectacular? Be willing to risk it.

Barbie Wins

I went to school with a woman who was a marketing whiz. She really wanted to get a job with Mattel, and she lined up an interview. She went in with "Barbie." She sat Barbie on the chair next to her and con-ducted the interview through Barbie. "Barbie says she would do x, y, and z in that situation." She took a risk...and landed the job.

Sometimes when you take a risk, the door opens. "WOW! An open door! A great sign!" you say. Then you walk through the door. It shuts. It is dark inside and you do not know your way around. Sounds like a typical risk to me. Panic could set in. Negative self-talk, "Why did I do this?" ya da ya da. It gets real scary. You might think you made a *Big* mistake.

Nonsense. You're in.

As long as you made sure the door you were going in was clearly marked "My new book" or "My dream business" etc., and not the federal prison, you'll be fine. Look for your sign on your risk door and walk through it.

Getting in, going through the darkness and through the challenges risk entails, is what matters. Someone on the other side of that door will light a candle and you will find the way. Sometimes they will even hold that door open for you. Halftime can be a chance to go through a different doorway, a better one. Regroup, risk, and choose. When you do get through the door, show 'em your best.

DON'T GET CAUGHT ON THE HOWS
FOCUS ON THE WOWS!

Risk Points You in the Right Direction

Always doing the safe thing is not the best way to stay safe.
Senator Orrin Hatch

Experimenting in life with what makes you "feel good" and gives you a natural high is the best way to your dreams. That dream was given to you, put inside you for you to uncover, figure out and use. Your dream is like David "trapped" inside the stone. Michelangelo had to uncover him by removing all that was not David. When you take a risk, your dream reveals itself to you. That is how life rewards you. Risk shows you the way.

The fearful are caught as often as the bold
Helen Keller

I watched a woman discourage speakers from trying out for a speakers' organization. "They were brutal on evaluations," she said. Anyone who showed an interest in expanding their speaking abilities would quickly be discouraged by the dragons she described waiting by the door of this speakers' organization. Yes, the evaluations were tough and seemed very cutting to a newcomer. But I sat and observed for a few months. Then, I timidly volunteered to speak and test the waters on a few simple things. I used the incredible speaking experience of the members gathered in that room and learned. I could see that the feedback was all designed to get the speaker where he or she needed to go to become a professional. It was a *gift* to the speaker. Not an insult.

By the time I was ready to give my qualifying speech, I had lots of support on my side, but I still had to give the speech. In getting ready, I accepted and created support wherever I could. Once I was up in front of my peers, on the firing line where the evaluations took place, it was different than I thought it would be.

Instead of appearing like bullets being fired at the poor speaker, the evaluations were precious nuggets of information as to how I could make my speech and "product" even more valuable to people. Instead of "cutting," the feedback was "sharp" and right on. I passed. The result is this book. My speech was called "Developing Your Inner Cheerleader."

QUESTION: What would I do if I didn't have to do it perfectly?

ANSWER: A great deal more than I am.
Julia Cameron

To do something spectacular, risk, and you will wow the crowd.

TAKE A RISK TO WOW
DO IT NOW!

The best halftimes are well-planned, highly prepared, spectacles that give the crowd the cheerleaders' absolute BEST!

The players are in the locker room, taking a much needed breather from the game. They are also devising new strategies for success and can't wait to get back to the game to implement their goal – to win!

So let's get back to the game
and see what else YOU can do to **win**.

www.yourinnercheerleader.com

Chapter 6

BACK TO THE GAME

You can't play not to lose – you have to play to win.
Bob Guiney

Your present circumstances don't determine where you can go;
they merely determine where you start.
Nido Qubein

BACK TO THE GAME

After entertainment or some time to rest, a cheerleader is ready again, refreshed, restrategized and wiser. An Inner Cheerleader has learned a lot from half a game. But there are more things Inner Cheerleaders do when they get back to the game.

1. WHEN YOU DO A STUNT, COMMIT 100 %

Whenever we totally commit ourselves, we are courageous.
David McNally

Comic Mel Brooks says his greatest piece of advice is, *If you walk up to the bell, you've got to ring it. In other words, no timid jokes, no nervous worrying...but just do it, loud and clear, ring the bell that your heart and your brains tell you to ring.*

One stunt required me to jump up and stand on another cheerleader's shoulders while she grabbed my ankles to hold me. I did not make it.

The captain of the squad was upset when I did not complete this stunt, and she made a very uncheerleaderlike statement: "You ruined the whole cheer." Should I have been upset about my performance? What if the base had been slightly off balance and was not ready to grab one of my legs as I jumped? I could have broken a leg, an ankle or even my neck if I had fallen. She could have been injured as well. Maybe my instincts protected both of us. Instead of embarrassing the crowd with one stunt, I may have saved us a disaster. I have chosen to look at it this way because there will be deals you need to pull out of when they feel wrong. Trust that.

The captain saw my "blowing it" as a failure. After that very same game someone came up to me and said, "You were out there cheering your heart out." Same game. Two people saw it differently. Who was right? Neither... or both? The important point of view here was mine. The one in front of my eyes. I knew I could not commit 100% to that stunt, so I did not do it.

Thus no chance for the planned "success," but the right decision for the circumstance.

Pulling back, as in the above example, is not the norm. Most of the time you can create a great chance for success, and in those instances you must be willing to commit 100%. If not, trust your feelings.

I've always believed that if you put in the work, the results will come.
I don't do things half-heartedly. Because I know if I do,
then I can expect half-hearted results."
Michael Jordon

The Lesson: Be willing to pull back if something is stopping you from committing 100%. But when you do commit, give your all.

2.   BE IN THE MOMENT

The present moment is the one point
where everything comes together.
Dr. Robert Anthony

Look not mournfully into the past.
It comes not back again.
Wisely improve the present. It is thine.
Henry Wadsworth Longfellow

A lot can happen quickly in a game. The business world has changed dramatically from a slow-moving game like baseball, to a game like football, with quick and driving action. Focus on the last play and where it now puts you in the game. Do not hang onto previous plays. That is the referee's job anyway.

You don't always get to make the calls. You *always* get to make the responses...the cheers. They are your choices, your creations.

To grow a business you will need some systems. From one call I make, I often need to make another two or three. Those calls then became two or more additional things to do. So the work actually increased with each step I took! It seemed the more work I did, the more work I created. How could I ever get ahead?

The way to handle a work overload is to ask, "What is the MOST important thing to do right now?" That is your focus. Which cheer? Cheerleaders do not do all the cheers at once, but the appropriate cheer for each moment.

Cheerleaders not only need to act in the present – *What should we do right now?* They need to calculate what to do for the immediate future – *Where do we want the team to be?* Think ahead, to get ahead. Speak as if you *are* ahead.

> *All of us tend to put off living.*
> *We are all dreaming of*
> *some magical rose garden over the horizon*
> *instead of enjoying the roses*
> *that are blooming outside our windows today.*
> Dale Carnegie

The present moment is like shifting binoculars into focus. Suddenly everything becomes clear.

EVERYTHING IS CLEAR
WHEN YOU STAY IN THE CHEER

3.   EVERY SECOND COUNTS

> *Perhaps the very best question that you can memorize and repeat,*
> *over and over is, "What is the most valuable use of my time right now?"*
> Brian Tracy

You know how important seconds are in sports. You can win or lose by the tiniest fraction of a second. Well, those little pieces of time are just as valuable in your life. What you do with EVERY second of your time does matter. Tremendously. Your life is *that* important.

It has been my observation that most people get ahead
during the time that others waste.
Henry Ford

4.   SPELL THINGS OUT FOR EXTRA IMPACT

Cheerleaders do not think the crowd is dumb. They do not deliver messages like attorneys or car salespeople on radio ads: *"Goteamgo-getatouchdownyoucandoitdoitagain!"*

They do not squeeze too much into their statements. Cheerleaders are not "auctioning" off the team. They allow each word to have full impact.

How can you spread success? Spell things out to people. Give them clear, strong details. Tie them together to make your point.

S   U   C   C   E   S   S
SPELL IT OUT TO GET SUCCESS

5.   CONNECT

It is only when one is connected to one's own core
that one is connected to others.
Anne Morrow Lindbergh

Cheerleaders are connectors. That is why they focus on the fans. They want to unite the fans and let the team hear that support. Cheerleaders are conductors. They conduct the orchestra. They get the music the fans create out onto the field so the players can hear it. If you get your audience and customers fired up, they will spread your message to a much larger arena. That is why you always keep them in focus.

Cheerleaders connect the crowd to the team and make it into a huge, powerful force. What are you connecting in your life? In your work?

The Lesson: Be a connector of people, of ideas.

It is Part of Life, Part of Our Nature to Cheer and Encourage

Over the years I have worked with and become friends with many Native Americans. Overall, they have done a wonderful job to keep their traditions alive and pure, in spite of many obstacles. In their celebrations and dances throughout the year, they cheer. They cheer to the clouds in the Cloud Dance. They cheer in the winter during the Deer Dance to encourage the deer to come out and give themselves up for the hunt. They see the hunt, not as a sport, but as a sacred part of the circle of life. They dance as a blessing for the people of the pueblo.

Cheerleaders bless the crowd and the team when they cheer for the win, the victory. The Native Americans have been doing this for centuries. How different is that from "GO TEAM GO!?"

6.   RESPECT THE TURF OF OTHERS

If you are good, you will be invited to play on a lot of different fields. Be grateful and respectful. When others are on your turf, be a generous and thoughtful host.

We had a game with a high school in Milwaukee, Wisconsin. They were a tough, inner-city crowd. In fact, it was rumored that their cheerleaders carried knives. Well, cheerleaders just didn't do those sorts of things, especially those from a little Midwestern town like ours.

Their players and cheerleaders were also much bigger than we were. We decided the best way to handle this was to make friends with them. We ignored the rumors. We were sister cheerleaders, each doing our best to promote our team. The result? We were rewarded with their friendship and an invitation to Milwaukee. We experienced that great feeling you get when you expand your world and go past stereotypes. Refuse to believe anything but the best about people. Oliver Wendell Holmes said it perfect, "A mind once expanded can never return to its original dimension."

7.   DON'T MIND THE ELEMENTS

There will always be some wind, some rain, some snow, and some heat. Like the postman delivering that mail, keep cheering for yourself no matter what the outside conditions are. The external conditions are not you. Your dreams are you. And you must be the first one to cheer them to life. Like the birds that sing the plants awake again in spring, cheer for yourself unconditionally.

The Right Elements

If you are inside a house, you dress for the indoors. If you go outside, you dress for the outdoors. Do you wear a winter coat inside if it is two degrees below outside? NO! It's 72 degrees inside, and the outside elements cannot affect you if you set the temperature inside to where you want it. Do not let the outside elements of life run your insides. We all have an internal *success* thermostat. Choose and set your own inside conditions for each area of your life.

Dream On

Just a dreamer. I was told I was just a dreamer. When I started on one of my film projects, I took the proposal to a former colleague for his advice. He was a man I sincerely respected. He discussed the project with me. Then he said that I was just a dreamer. Ouch! I could have believed him. I could have believed his thoughts and opinions were more valuable than mine.

I could have believed that I was ONLY a dreamer. Instead, I believed in those dreams. A big project came to life because of that dream.

The elements outside - his "opinion"- seemed dreary. I had to choose to not "mind" those elements. The outside elements do not control your mind unless you let them.

Raise the bar. Do not lower it. This is an upward-moving world. Those who do not go up will be left below the line.

The World Is Big Enough to Fit Your Dreams Into It

The world is all gates, all opportunities,
strings of tension waiting to be struck.
Ralph Waldo Emerson

When people tell you that you cannot do something and you have thought of them as being smarter, more experienced, or any stature higher than you, you must raise yourself ABOVE the place you gave them in order to achieve your dream. They have given you a gift, if you can see it that way. To get yourself to that new dream, you will have to grow "up" to reach it.

You climb the rope of success. You start alone if you have to. The rope is there. Use it. Others may come along and climb with you. Some people will be able to pull you up, if they choose to. Do not let them pull you down. Grab that rope and go! For Pete's sake, don't hang yourself with it.

GO ABOVE THE CLOUDS
TO GET ABOVE THE CROWD

8.   LOVE EVERY MINUTE OF THE GAME

You have to find something that you love
enough to be able to take risks,
jump over the hurdles and
break through the brick walls
that are always going to be
placed in front of you.
If you don't have that kind of feeling
for what it is you're doing,
you'll stop at the first giant hurdle.
George Lucas

Love every moment of the game...or do not play. Pick a new game, but *Love* the game you chose.

Like the amazing moment standing by the fence at a football game that I described in the front of the book, I *Loved* the cheering feeling so much that it was always new and exciting to me. Every part of the game was wonderful. You can have a game that gives you that much pleasure. I am sure of it.

Live every moment to the fullest, and you will *Love* every moment. Use the sights, sounds, and the smells that exist all around you to create a rich experience and *Love every* moment.

You think Bill Gates *Loves* the game? He probably gets up each morning cheering:

WITH EACH BIT AND BYTE THEY MAKE...
A LOT OF MONEY TO THE BANK I TAKE.

When I go to my office every morning,
I feel like I am going to the Sistine Chapel to paint.
Warren Buffett

9.   DO ONLY ONE CHEER AT A TIME

Cheerleaders do not confuse the crowd with too many messages. Cheers are quick, clear and focused. Even if you have a stack of "absolutely must get done now" things, you can only do one at a time. Start with one. Just one. Give it all of your attention. Then move onto the next. Give that all your attention. That is how some of the biggest things in the world, such as skyscrapers, get made.

The Power of One

Being an Aries, I tended to have 50 projects going on at once. I would feel overwhelmed and get frustrated. Nothing would get done until I learned that when I start to feel overwhelmed, focus on one thing at a time. Stay with it until it gets done. Handle the discomfort of all the other unfinished things by pushing them out of your mind. Give full attention to just one task.

Imagine a line at the bank. The teller would not say, "Hey, you in the green shirt, I know you need to cash that check - just bring it here. OK, you in the blue suit, let me start working on your money order. Lady, you with the baby in your arms, let me check on your account balance." No, he takes it step by step, customer by customer, transaction by transaction.

Do not take them all at once. Put your full attention into one, then into the next. Forget multitasking, or you'll end up like Lucille Ball in the Chocolate Factory scene.

Focus Pocus

Distractions during your working day - emails, phone calls, etc. - are like driving to your destination and stopping and looking at every advertising sign along the way. You would NEVER get there. You have to decide to keep going to reach your goal and follow YOUR plan to YOUR destination.

10.   DON'T MAKE EXCUSES

A cheerleader's goal is to help the team win. They are focused and clear. A cheerleader would not make any of the following statements about a receiver who did not catch the ball.

"John did not make that pass because:

a) "He was out late last night with the boys."

b) "He was out late last night with the girls."

c) "He has a hangover."

Oh, really. We do not need to know. Just play ball.

If John did not make the pass, a cheerleader cheers him on anyway. Again. Over and over. That is what you must do for yourself. No matter what happens. Over and over.

A cheerleader's job is not to focus on the reasons why people do or do not do something, but to cheer them further along, toward success.

In business, an Inner Cheerleader does not focus on all the reasons why she did not make that last sale. Instead, she would tell herself, "You have a new customer now... make your pitch again. But pitch even better this time."

The Inner Cheerleader does not confuse reasons and encouragement. If a cheerleader is cheering "Defense. Defense," and the other team makes a touchdown, the cheerleader did not do the wrong cheer. She does not blame herself for that touchdown. She has no direct connection to an outcome she didn't choose, only her connection to keep encouraging the team to go for the win. The cheerleader is not accountable for the results of the play, but responsible for encouraging the players to *make* the play. That is what you can do for yourself. Reach inside to tackle your problems. Inside is where the

Inner Cheerleader can help you. Be accountable to yourself for your own motivation, for cheering yourself to success.

When success comes, you will *have* to say "No" to more opportunities than you say "Yes" to. Do not make excuses for that. Do not get stuck on the reasons. Focus on results. Just keep choosing those things that will help you win. But do not get stuck on them either.

DO NOT USE
AN EXCUSE

11.   WHEN CHEERING, LOOK UP - NOT DOWN

The crowd is above - in the bleachers, not in the basement. Cheerleaders have to raise their sights to encourage that crowd.

DON'T LOOK DOWN, DON'T WEAR A FROWN
BECAUSE WAY UP HIGH, IS WHERE DREAMS FLY

My father always cheers me up. His unique sense of humor and outrageous puns have helped me to look up when I feel down. From his quip,

"What do you see when you look down? ...De feet." to

"I always look up, because when I look down I can't see my feet... my belly's in the way."

Don't you believe that! But it sure made me laugh. So keep your head up high, and aim for the sky.

NeuroLinguistic Programming (NLP) states that if you lower your eyes to look directly at anything or anyone, your memory will go blank. A completely downcast eye position is associated with past events. How powerful it is when we decide where to put our focus! You literally carry your past with you if your eyes are looking down, instead of looking directly into the present. Why not look up into your bright new future too? The one you create with your beautiful new thoughts.

There is a wonderful quote in *Ski* Magazine about the skiing style of the great champion Stein Eriksen: "Skiing so effortless it seemed to require only beautiful thoughts." Have beautiful thoughts in your life and you will create your beautiful life.

AIM YOURSELF HIGH
SET YOUR GOALS FOR THE SKY

12.   SOMETIMES YOU JUST HAVE TO FLOAT

Floating Can Save Your Life

Cheerleaders "float" through the air during their stunts. They also make and decorate the floats for parades. They ride on those floats, cheering and waving.

When things get heavy and it feels like you are drowning and can't swim anymore, relax... float. Let someone else drive. You smile and wave.

It doesn't matter how deep the water is if you are floating.
John Harricharan

My dad told me to "float" when life gets tough. Just float. When you float, you are at the point between the air and the water. At the boundary between two worlds. Float through life. You will travel more lightly than if you trudge. You are still close to the ground, but you don't have to worry about tripping on every pebble. And your shoes last longer! Floating is rising above things. When you are floating on the water long-term, what direction are you facing? UP! You better be. Face down is not a good thing.

WHEN THERE'S NO BOAT
JUST FLOAT

Reframe

Another way to look at something is to reframe it. Get a bigger or different frame. If the picture you see is giving you a negative feeling, put it into a larger, better or more concise frame. That can help. Love enlarges the frame you put around things.

A little boy was bouncing all over the seat next to mine at a restaurant. I said to myself, "Thank God I did not sit on that side of the booth." Then I realized my thought probably was not the highest one I could think. What would be a better one? Suppose I thought: "Wow, does that kid have energy! There must be a lot of life force flowing through him." A much better feeling spread through my body, and I began to appreciate that little bundle of spirit called a boy, instead of being annoyed with him.

REFRAME: If you don't like one picture, cover a portion of it or get a larger one. Make the part you do not like a very small element in a very large picture like Waldo in "Where's Waldo? In other words, look at it a different way.

REFRAME YOUR GAME,
AND IT'S NOT THE SAME

13. IF YOU WANT TO ATTRACT ATTENTION, GET OUT ON THE FIELD

You were not created to be small...but to be big. Big like Life.
John Assaraf

Use Something to Catch People's Attention

Cheerleaders use a short skirt and a smile to get attention. What will you use? The SMILE...cannot hurt.

Take on life. Get in the game. Get out there on the field. Show your stuff. Let life know who you are.

GO YOU!

You will have more chances for success the more you get out in life, the more you are seen. Try different arenas, all playing fields. If you start winning on one field, keep going to that field. If not, try other fields. You will find your winning field. Trust. There is a field for every one of you.

GET OUT IN LIFE AND MAKE THE ROUNDS
THAT IS WHERE SUCCESS IS FOUND

14.   SMILE

Everyone is hungry for a friendly face. When I tried out for cheer-leading I was told to smile no matter what - even if I looked like a Cheshire cat.

Happiness is a habit. Put a smile on the inside.
Joy starts with a decision.
Greg Anderson

Million-Dollar Smile?

There was a time I believe I may have had a million-dollar smile. My office was located across from a conference room. My boss was holding an important meeting with a potential donor who had recently lost her husband. When the woman came out of that room looking kind of lost and sad, I looked up and gave her a warm smile. The next day she donated $1 million. My boss told us right after that meeting that he thought it had gone terribly. But on the way out of that room, maybe it was the little smile she remembered and took home with her that warmed her heart. Who knows if that smile made a real difference? Most people don't smile nearly enough.

Are you smiling right now? Smile - because you are alive!

Smile and the whole world smiles with you. A smile almost always requires a reciprocal. You smile. They WHAT? Smile! Did you ever see a cheerleader frown? Who would follow her? You can hear a smile over the phone. Others can tell. Smile with your eyes.

The Eye Smile

My mom, bless her heart, had me practice doing this when I was a cheerleader. I covered my mouth with my hands and asked her:

"Am I smiling with my eyes now?"
"No," she said.
"How about now?"
I kept practicing until I got it.

What a gift she gave me! It is even more valuable because today my mother is blind.

Smile on your phone calls. If no one is around to smile to, smile at yourself in a mirror. It is a little pick-me-up. They say you need 10 hugs a day. Maybe you need at least 10 smiles a day to remain positive. Give them to yourself. Then give the rest of your smiles away.

Remember. It is a game! HAVE F U N!!!

15.   CHEER FOR THE TEAM YOU ARE GIVEN

It can be unpleasant to play on a team
with people whom you don't like. But it makes you smarter.
Gail Evans

Ninety-eight percent of the time, your team will come "as is." You will not get to pick it. If you are given a less-than-winning team, sometimes you can encourage the group to rise by your higher level of expectations for them. Be proud to cheer for the team you are given.

We had a great football team my junior year of high school. The next year the school split into two schools, East and West. The best players were on the older, well-established East Side. That team was developed together and had worked out together. The new West Side team did not have enough time to integrate players and styles. Our team often lost. In my high school, I could not choose the players. Often, you cannot either.

But every once in a while you do get to pick out or create your team. For example, a good director gets to choose at least most of his team for his movie. If given the opportunity to do so, how do you choose a good team?

My own way is to look at the level of passion someone has. Also look at the level of love they have. Which players have the most love? How much does each player hold onto fear? Throw out all the fear in your decisions. What will be left, is the love.

A winning team has to have the courage to let go of fear or at least be willing to walk through it. Nothing new will be accomplished with fear. The world needs new ways of doing things.

Be one of those who will lead. Choose people who are not afraid of their fears to work with you.

We define people by age, not by uniqueness. For example, the news refers to the 59-year-old so-and- so, rather than "the person who devoted his life to the preservation of tigers with his gentle touch."

We see people by the ages of their bodies. We need to see people by the ages of their minds, their emotions and their ability to love. Then we can make better choices about the people we surround ourselves with.

CHEER FOR THOSE WHO SURROUND YOU
THEIR SUCCESS WILL GROW ALL AROUND YOU

16. WHAT DO CHEERLEADERS DO? THEY YELL. YELL LOUD!

People don't read memos, but they'll listen to a big mouth.
Barbara Corcoran

What is a cheerleader's favorite drink? ROOT BEER

What is a cheerleader's favorite color? YELLER

Their job is not just to yell, but to get the audience to yell. Eight or ten girls yelling, multiplied by the audience, all in unison, inspires the team. Yes, it is only one part of being a cheerleader, but they put out energy in a big way. They have enthusiasm and passion. Through their gestures and their smiles, they rouse the fans. Apply this to business. Your customers are the fans. Your business is the team. Get the fans (customers) to yell for the business. You yell to the fans. They yell to the team. The team wins. The fans create the action that will help your team succeed.

Put your spirit, your life breath, into it. Use movement and action. If you say "go team go," is it going to happen? Not likely. Tell yourself **GO!** Others will get the message you are serious.

Do not cheer... "Go team go. Oh I have to call these people. Oh I have to do this report."

NO!

Cheer this: "**YAHOO! I GET TO MAKE THIS GREAT REPORT! HOW CAN I MAKE IT EVEN BETTER?**"

It sounds like such a simple, obvious thing, but most people talk to themselves this way. If you'll cheer yourself **THIS WAY**, the change in your life will be profound.

What do you tell yourself regarding your life, your business dealings? Are you enthusiastic? If not, why would your customers buy or even listen to you? I have taped my side of conversations when I was in a business slump so I could see how my energy is coming across. The energy was low. My voice sounded like a car that was hardly moving. What a revealing exercise!

Get yourself on a fun ride through life. Make your life work. Act like it is fun, and it will start to be more fun. Remember Mark Twain's Tom Sawyer? He got help painting the fence by pretending it was fun. Tom Sawyer knew how to motivate.

The best way to cheer yourself up is to cheer someone else up.
Mark Twain

Sing Hallelujah!

My Uncle Butch is not afraid of his voice. One morning in church the pastor asked the audience, "Do you want to sing or do you want to leave?" Uncle Butch thought the whole congregation would respond, so he said as loud as he could: **"Sing!"** However, the pastor was asking a rhetorical question. The audience remained silent as Uncle Butch's voice was the only one answering loud and clear, **"Sing!"** in that church. Uncle Butch just happened to be sitting next to the pastor's wife. My Aunt Lynn wanted to hide under the bench. It only takes a little instigation for my uncle to sing "Hallelujah!" Why not you?

17. YOU ARE ALWAYS ON DISPLAY, EVERY WORD, EVERY ACTION

So act like it. You have a choice to cheer in almost every given moment. Your brain hears everything you think. Your thoughts are like books for your brain. Read good ones.

You are going to be on display. Being in the limelight might have some consequences. So what? Present your best self anyway.

When I was in high school, a rumor spread that one of the cheerleaders was pregnant. It was baseless, but how would she deny it? Luckily, time was on her side. She just had to wait a few months. Not everything is this easy, though.

In business, many people will start rumors. Some are worth fighting. Some are best ignored. Rise above. Ignore most rumors and they will quickly die.

18.   SHARE RESPONSIBILTY

Whenever a cheerleader sees an opportunity for a cheer, she starts cheering. The others join in. They do not compete. The competition is on the field, not in the ranks of true cheerleaders. They know that they are more effective as a squad.

Whoever sees the opportunity first, goes for it. But a cheerleader needs the support of the others when she starts a cheer. She knows she will get it.

In business, when you work with people, allow them as much room as you can. Let them start their own cheers because they will, in effect, be cheering for your company.

Take turns - just like your mother may have told you. Let others cheer too.

19.   THE IMPORTANT WHICH YOU DO
IS IN THINGS ORDER

Yes, I really am speaking English. You will understand it if I write it this way...

The Order in Which You Do Things Is Important

As an example, a given math problem may seem very complicated at first. However, by first breaking the problem down into smaller steps, then by prioritizing those steps, even a seemingly complex problem can be solved fairly easily.

Here is a seemingly challenging problem: (4-3.5) (5+24) + 8/2-3x2. The first step is to break the problem into smaller steps, by placing the numbers into logical groups. Solve within the parenthesis first. That makes the multiplication easier. After you break into groups and simplify within groups, you then multiply, then divide, then add the remaining pieces.

By focusing on this problem as a whole, it might be easy to get overwhelmed and may result in a wrong solution. By attacking the problem in pieces, individual tasks seem easier and more often lead to accuracy. In life, our problems are not always easy to figure out. But sometimes just getting the right order is how we can solve them. Begin by taking only one workable step at a time.

Smack in the Middle

What happens in the middle of the month, in every season except summer? It happens only in the night and never in the day? To answer the brainteaser, think very logically, one step at a time.

Step one: the middle of the month. Hmmm. That would have to be the letter "n."

And the letter "n" fits all the other requirements.

Easy... if you take it one step at a time.

(My friend Brian Adams gave me that brainteaser)

If you are redoing the carpet and someone gave you all the steps but mixed them up as follows, you'd have a mess:

1. Remove the carpet.
2. Remove the pad.

3. Put in the carpet.

4. Put in the pad.

But if you know the steps and the order, and do step 4 before step 3, you can get it right.

On a lock combination of 33, 55, 25, if the correct order is 33, left three times, 55 right two times then to 25, the lock will not open until you get it perfect. Sometimes your life lessons are like that. You have to get the lesson perfect and then the reward beyond the safe is yours. Note I said beyond the "safe." That goes back to the willingness to risk.

Cheerleaders take one step at a time. They do the right cheer at the right time. They warm up the crowd. They do pre-game cheers. Then they do offensive or defensive cheers. Later they do time-out cheers. Next they do their halftime entertainment. Finally, they always try to leave the crowd feeling good about the team and the game - no matter what the outcome.

Ace the Pace

Have you ever noticed? Anybody going slower than you is an idiot, and anyone going faster than you is a maniac.
George Carlin

I had a large hill behind my home that I used to walk down. Once I ran down the hill at the start of my daily walk. It felt great running downhill. I covered more ground a lot quicker. But I still had my whole walk ahead of me *and* the *uphill* climb on the way back. Never did that again!

A lot of businesses start out this way. They are gung ho. And all their energy goes into the start. But where businesses succeed, where they make it or break it, is on the long haul. Save enough energy for that long walk and do not burn it up all at once. Do not make a big bonfire when a steady fire will keep you warm longer.

Cheerleaders do not do all their best cheers and routines right at the start. They know the crowd will need a little fuel later on, and they give it to them. Save some energy so you can make it to those last important cheers.

Moderate effort over a long time is important,
no matter what you are trying to do.
One brings failure on oneself by working
extremely hard at the beginning,
attempting to do too much,
and then giving it all up after a short time.
The Dalai Lama

20.   BE WILLING TO MAKE THE CALL

I'm indecisive. No doubt about it!
Bob Lee

Good judgment comes from experience,
experience comes from bad judgment.
Mark Twain

A referee has to be willing to make the call, or the winner would never be decided. You need to make the calls that will move you to victory. Those calls have to be the most honest and best calls you can make.

Sometimes you have to make the best call you can under pressure. That's what a real leader has to do, like it or not. A ref does not say, "Oh, I'm not sure. Let me think about it." The players would tackle him!

Make the best call you can, but make it.

21.   IT'S NEVER TOO LATE TO WIN

I find that every big success happens after
I think I've exhausted 100% of my options.
For me success happened only after I gave another 10%.
Barbara Corcoran

It is never too late to win once you know it's possible. Look at me. I'm not an 18 year-old cheerleader anymore. Darn! The point is, the Inner Cheerleading tool did not present itself fully to me until much later in life. Success can come at any point along the line if you keep moving toward it.

I was always afraid of things that worked the first time.
Thomas A. Edison

You Can Be More Than You Think You Are

Anything in life can come any time in the game. What if you found out you were a twin? That happened to my dad when he was in his 60's. His father took him aside one day and told him. My dad really had difficulty believing it at first, yet others in the family had been told. Back then they didn't mention things like a baby dying at birth. What a secret!

For years my dad had been telling everyone the world couldn't take another one like him. Then he found out the truth. He was one of two!

IT'S NEVER TOO LATE
TO LEAVE THE GATE

22.   WITHOUT ACTION YOU DO NOT WIN

As you pray, move your feet.
Quaker saying

Cheerleaders cheer. The team plays. They win or they do not win. But to win, they had to DO something. The players had to be willing to take an action – to run, throw the ball, make the pass, tackle the player – in order to win. The team does not just sit on the sidelines wishing to win, thinking about winning. They play. They act. And because of that, at least one team does win. And the other team learns something in the process that hopefully will help them win next time.

Take affirmative action. I'm not talking about the political term. An affirmative action is a positive action directed toward your goal. Cheers work like magic, but a practical magic that you can use in your life to create amazing results. Affirming the results by taking action helps to create the results. Writing coach Lee Pound says: "When we take a physical action, we break the inertia. When you are blocked, just start doing something. Make it start. Make it flow."

23. CHEERS CLEANSE THE SUBCONSCIOUS

Cheers go directly into the subconscious because our minds like rhymes and upbeat messages. Brains like learning this way. Cheers are actually simple and childlike. Our minds do not censor them as much. Plus cheers are a lot of fun to do. Rah, Rah! Go Go! They are not drudgery or a chore. They are entertainment.

To alter your life in a good and fun way is delightful. Change does not have to be so hard.

Cheers use the visual, auditory and kinesthetic parts of your learning systems. The chance to have one of these get through to your subconscious where change occurs is much higher, especially if you really raise the energy, smile, and have fun.

Congratulations! By now you have looked over a large number of strategies you can use to create more success. You have learned a lot from the way a cheerleader goes through the game. Pick the cheer strategies that resonate with you and try them for a month. By then you may want to try out a few more.

It's after the game, now what? And by the way...

CONGRATULATIONS, YOU'RE ALMOST DONE
YOU'VE GONE THROUGH THE GAME
HOPE YOU HAD FUN!

It's just another day.
It's just another play
in the great game of life.

Chapter 7

AFTER THE GAME

*It's a very good plan every now and then
to go away and have a little relaxation.
When you come back your judgment will be surer,
since to remain constantly at work will
cause you to lose the power of judgment.*
Leonardo da Vinci

www.yourinnercheerleader.com

AFTER THE GAME

When the game is finished, cheerleaders look at the results. From those results, they can make corrections and do things differently next time if they need to. Or they can do more of the things that worked well. Cheerleaders know that certain mindsets are important to have after the game. Here they are.

1. THERE IS ALWAYS ANOTHER GAME - UNLESS IT'S THE PLAYOFFS

If you are successful in regular games, you'll get a shot at the playoffs. Know the difference between the playoffs and regular games. Every game is important, but some games count more for your success. Figure out which areas of your business are your playoffs. Is it a phone call to a key contact or to a distributor? Put your first and your best efforts there. We know we should do this, but we often do not. Give the ball to your best players. Which are the regular games and which are the playoffs in your life?

You have all heard of the 80/20 rule: 80% of a business's profits come from 20% of its customers. What is 80 but a B! And a low B, at that.

I am going to offer another rule. I believe in 95/5. Go for the 5%. You get an A and all kinds of doors open. The book *The Tipping Point* by Malcolm Gladwell describes this.

THE PLAYOFFS
ARE THE PAYOFFS
And they require more focus.

2. AFTER THE GAME, GO OUT FOR PIZZA AND ROOT BEER

Hash over the game, bond, laugh and let go.

Reward yourself, whether it is pizza or root beer. Whether you take yourself or your employees to a spa or a golf course, after the game, play and just have fun.

THE GAME IS DONE

GO HAVE SOME FUN

After the game is done, you want to be able to sit around with the great friends you played the game with and say, "That was terrific! What a GREAT game!"

Celebrate the game, take a little break, then come back and look at what you have learned from playing that game. Cheerleaders not only learn from their own performances, but from observing others play the game.

Chapter 8

WHAT YOU CAN LEARN
FROM WATCHING THE GAME

Opportunity is abundant which means there is a game
for all those who truly want to play.
David McNally

www.yourinnercheerleader.com

WHAT YOU CAN LEARN FROM
WATCHING THE GAME

1.　BE A GOOD RECEIVER

You cannot be successful without learning how to receive. As you learn to receive more, you learn to give more. You really can't do one without the other. Even a football player has to receive the ball before he can score or give the ball to someone else who can. No team could possibly win without receiving. When you can open up to receiving more good things, it is amazing. More of them start to show up in your life.

2.　WHEN YOU FALL DOWN, GET UP

Not many people are willing to give failure a second opportunity.
They fail once and it is all over.
The bitter pill of failure is often more than most people can handle.
If you are willing to accept failure and learn from it,
if you are willing to consider failure
as a blessing in disguise and bounce back,
you have got the essence of harnessing
one of the most powerful success forces.
Joseph Sugarman

How many times in a game do you see a 250- or 300-pound guy fall down? Dozens, even hundreds. How many times do they get back up? Almost always.

They get hit hard. They do not waste any time. They get up and play again so they can reach their goal.

Those who pick themselves up after defeat
and keep on trying, arrive;
and the world cries,
"Bravo! I knew you could do it!"
Napoleon Hill

3. THE HUDDLE IS A STILL POINT

When things are moving too fast and not going where you want them to go, take a break and get into a huddle. The huddle is a fetal position for the team. It is a fresh starting point. A back-to-our-mission point. A focus circle.

Several years ago it seemed as though my life was at a standstill. Nothing seemed to be moving. Jobs weren't working out, income from CDs had dried up, mailings and sales produced meager results; even some of my relationships dried up like a pond after a severe drought - until I put my house on the market. This brought in a whole new energy. I got still, went into a huddle in my mind, and realized that I did not like where I lived. My home situation was affecting *everything* in my life. I was demotivating myself living there.

Like a car that was being driven around in reverse, my life was not going anywhere in a place that did not nurture me. Once *I* got still, things in my life started to move! Literally. By putting the car in park or neutral, you can switch gears and go forward in the right direction. That still point allowed me the focused energy I needed to make the necessary course correction.

It is especially powerful when you can go into a huddle with others who have the same goal as you do. Then the huddle is extra focused energy toward a common goal. But even alone, going into a huddle gives *you* great focused energy. The huddle is like a bull's-eye. You bring everything in to a center point, which will greatly increase your scoring potential.

4. EVEN WHEN A GOAL SEEMS LIKE THE LONG WAY HOME...KEEP GOING

Cheerleaders learn from the game that sometimes those with the longest, most impossible-looking tasks will make the most dramatic, exciting and inspiring plays. Plays that people will talk about for years.

In the game of life it is sometimes those with the most difficult beginnings who seem to accomplish what others think miraculous. They inspire us.

Life does not always seem to make sense. Some people appear to have it easy, others have it hard. It is as if we each parachuted from an airplane with instructions to go to a certain location. Some have a very difficult journey to take. They are dropped far, far away from their destination. Others may know where they have to go, but they may not know how to get there. And some seemed to be dropped right on their target destination. They appear to have an easy life.

Many of us don't know yet where our "dream" destination is. Your first step is to know your goal. Then the next step is taking the journey to get there. Wherever you are on that journey, it's OK. It does not matter WHERE you are on the path to your destination as long as you keep going for it. If you get knocked down on the field of life, you get up and make the next play. If you get pushed back to your own 1-yard line, you dig in and plunge forward to the other team's end zone. You will know when you reach your destination. We cheer for those in life who get up and go forward even when pushed back.

5. THERE IS RARELY A STRAIGHT AND NARROW PATH

Where? Where is there a straight and narrow path? Not in sports. Rarely in nature, even the horizon is curved. When a butterfly goes from Point A to Point B, there are thousands of points it touches to get there. Your goal may take you down a seemingly random path, but if you have got that goal "in mind" you'll get there, just like the butterfly that makes a beautiful pattern in the air on its journey.

Once in a great while, a football player can run straight for a touchdown, but usually he has to detour around many obstacles to get to his goal. That's what makes the game exciting and unpredictable. That makes a determined, unstoppable player. That makes a hero.

As I was taking a walk, a butterfly got in front of me. It flew here and there and all over while still going forward. I liked the message the beautiful little creature gave me to give to you: In going forward, dance.

Your dreams will not always lie on the straight path. Like that charming little butterfly, you can make beautiful patterns on the way to your dreams.

IF YOU GET A "NO"
GO WHERE THERE'S A FLOW

6.   STAY OUT OF THE WAY OF THE BALL

The ball has its own energy and direction. Team members must let it continue on its path, unless they see a clear opening for an interception or it lands somewhere.

When it appears that the ball is going to go out of bounds, the players just let it fall.

In ancient Rome, two powerful men were vying for the title of emperor. Cleopatra waited until it was clear that Marc Anthony, not Octavius, would have the power. She let the "ball" of Roman power take its own course. But when it settled - she was all over it. That's when she made her historical move... to seduce Marc Anthony.

The important point for the team is to know where the ball is at all times. Then they can make the appropriate move. If it is going out of bounds, they do not touch it. They let it die. It will reincarnate at a better spot than if they'd wasted all that energy trying to catch it.

STAND TALL
AND LET THE BALL FALL

Cleo was a great player. She knew where the ball was and never let that ball out of her sight until the play was over. The ball is the action of business. The momentum. Just stand square.

The Lesson: Know when your side has the ball.

Sometimes You Have to Just Wait for Your Moment

I was asked to speak at an annual convention. First, I was asked to give a short speech. While gathering more information on the event, I was informed that I would be on a panel instead. Since being on a panel is much easier to prepare for than a speech, I didn't really prepare much. However, the day before I left for the trip, they said I would be giving a speech instead. Ahhhh! To top it off, I did not really know exactly what they wanted me to speak about, the order, the length, the location and a few other details most speakers like to know before speaking. I was more than a little nervous about that! During the dinner at the event, the Emcee came up to me and said, "We are running late. I'll only have time to introduce you after all."

My thoughts quickly flew from a bit of relief, to disappointment that I could not address my peers, and finally landed in the following cheering self-talk: "I'll just go with the flow. I will get my chance. If not now, it will happen."

My mind was doing what I call the "pinball machine effect." That is when my thoughts keep jumping around. Eventually they settle in one of several slots with different point values. Wouldn't you know about 15 minutes later, I heard the Emcee describing a person who sounded extremely similar to me! Then I heard my name being called and asked to come up front and give a speech. I do not believe that I would have been asked to speak to that wonderful crowd if I had held a grudge and been in a bad mood. The energy I put out in that room would have been different.

> LET THE BALL FALL
> THEN MAKE THE CALL

Ball playing is thinking. So is business. Cleo knew. If she played too soon, she could have lost the guy with power. She just decided to hang back, eat grapes and let the ball fall.

7. A GOOD COACH WILL CALL A TIME-OUT AT A CRITICAL POINT AND REFOCUS THE PLAYERS

One of my favorite comments by a coach was that of Donald G. Lessner, Bob "The Bachelor" Guiney's high school football coach. After Guiney made a great touchdown, he was so excited he started pumping his fist wildly in the air. After the game, his coach played him that footage over and over and said, "Hey, Guiney. Do me a favor. Next time, make it look like you've been there before."

A good coach can see when and where a little guidance is needed. Guiney's coach took him aside for a time-out that would profoundly affect Guiney.

A good coach knows when the team needs to refocus. His timing can determine a win or a loss. The good coach knows the players and the game well enough to say, "Let's come together and get motivated." Can you spot when you need a time-out? When you've been driving forward and start to lose sight of the goal, or if you become so scattered that you have forgotten why you are working so hard, call a time-out. Talk to others. Take yourself briefly out of the game and when you get back in, your energy will be higher and your focus clearer. You will have to make those calls in your own life. Know when it is critical to do so.

Some players I had to pat on the back a lot...
and then there were others
that I had to pat a little lower and a little harder.
Coach John R. Wooden

Coaches need Inner Cheerleaders too, because they have to make important decisions on the spot. Who cheers for the coaches? Who cheers them up? They have learned to cheer for themselves. People expect coaches to cheer for the team. "Come on, Coach, give us a great strategy," they yell. "What can we do to win, Coach?" they plead. A good coach provides guidance. We do not always cheer for leaders, such as coaches, so coaches need to have a highly developed Inner Cheerleader who keeps them focused on their goals.

During a critical period in your life – and we all have those – take a time-out. I believe we make up for lost time anyway, especially if we are taking good care of ourselves by doing what we need to do in that moment. Use your good judgment and use your time. It is yours.

8. LET GO OF THE OLD GAME... EMBRACE THE NEW ONE

Through the years the game changes. The old talent leaves, the new talent comes in. This is how the game grows. We often miss the old players, but we can start to get interested in the new players and why they were given a chance to be on that field. There's usually a good reason.

9. YOU CAN'T CHEER EVERYONE UP

Don't waste your energy on someone who wants to be miserable. Some people aren't ready for happiness yet.

Just let them be. Not everyone wants to be cheered up and you will remain happier yourself if you allow them to be miserable.

A woman attending one of my seminars had an excuse for every positive thing I suggested to her. She batted them all away as quickly as I gave them to her. I finally decided I was spending too much time helping her get to a positive state, when the man next to her was really receptive. I silently blessed her and moved my focus to where my energy was being accepted.

Others may not always accept your cheeriness, but remember, cheers will make YOU a happier person

10.   AIM FOR YOUR GOAL POST

When you write down your goal, it becomes an affirmation.
Dr. Robert Anthony

Do You Set Weekly Goals or Do You Set Goals Weakly?

In life I always wanted to go for the touchdown. I always knew where I wanted to be and where I believed I needed to go, but the distance seemed so great I thought I could only win by scoring a touchdown. I did not realize then that it was the smaller, day-to-day goals that got me to the end zone. Being upset at not being at the 0-yard line when it appears you are still at your own 20-yard line doesn't get you there. A step at a time does.

Stepping in Thin Air

I had a unique experience with a man. He fell out of the sky and landed on me. Never saw him before. Never saw him since. Just one split second in time, when I looked up and saw him about to land on me, which he did.

It happened on a bright sunny day while I was standing in the middle of the street. My alma mater was having a sign unveiling. They had received word that they were accredited to become a university. I was invited to the ceremony, which took place near a little patch of grass in front of the covered sign. As they unveiled the sign, unbeknownst to the audience, a plane flew over and dropped out several members of a National Skydiving Team. The first skydiver landed on the tiny lawn as we cheered with lots of fanfare. Then I turned around to see the next skydiver, but what I saw instead was boots. Big Boots. Pedaling wildly to get more air. Instinctively I turned away as the boots hit and we both ended up in a pile on the street. Amazingly, I was not hurt. Even more amazing, my red silk suit was not ripped, or damaged. My nylons were blackened from the street but that was it.

Once I got back up and shook myself off, I reviewed the situation and decided to go over to the young man. He was visibly shaken because he had just missed his target and landed on people instead. Offering my hand I said to him, "I think you had better at least introduce yourself." Today, I cannot remember his name, only those circling boots as he took steps of air to try and reach his "goal post."

Your goal post will probably not be as difficult to land on as his was. You will most likely be able to take solid steps to reach it. Do so. And just a note of advice - if there are going to be skydivers around...don't wear red!

How Many Cheers Will You Need To Do?

Well, that depends. From one formed belief, you made thousands, perhaps millions, of subconscious decisions; decisions that still affect every area of your life. EVERYTHING! How many cheers will you have to do? A more important question is how much more of your life will you waste going in a direction you no longer want to go? If you find out you have been driving to Alaska when you wanted to go to Florida, TURN AROUND. It really is as simple as choosing a different direction.

But you have to catch yourself every time you start driving back to Alaska and return to the direction in which you want to go.

If you don't do your cheers, it's like buying a new car and never driving it. It might be great to look at, but unless you get in it and use it, it can never take you anywhere.

Don't expect to do just one cheer and think that's it. That's like laying one brick for a building and saying, "Sorry, but this is no building. This brick doesn't work." Of course it does! It's the first step toward a building of thousands of bricks, depending on how big you want to go. You place another brick and another, and pretty soon you have the structure. That's how you build success. Take consistent action toward your goals and you will get there. Cheers are actions. They place an order for a goal each time you cheer.

Let your cheers lead you to where you want to go.

Now, how do you put all this together to create a cheering program to take you to your goal line - the success you want?

In addition to doing your morning cheers, the following actions put what cheerleaders have learned into a more concise strategy.

CHEERS IN ACTION

Examples and Tips to Bring Cheers into Your Life

- **Send a Cheer-a-gram**

Leave cheery notes. When my daughter was growing up, I left "cheery" notes for her. Notes like "Have a wonderful day." or "You did great." That sort of thing. Later, when she was older, she started to do that for me. When I went on trips, my suitcase was full of little messages like "Nikki (our dog) and I will miss you" or "Have a fantastic trip." What a beautiful way to uplift another! After she moved out, I had no one to write cheery notes for me. I am sure I felt sorry for myself about this for a while.

Finally, I decided that it was OK to do it for myself. It would have the same effect - perhaps an even greater effect - because it would be specifically what I wanted. At least once a week, I write myself a cheery note. This motivates me and also shows appreciation for the work I do and the effort I make. Someone cares. I do. Self-acknowledgment is important.

One of the best notes I left for myself, I wore. When I first started public speaking, I was nervous, as most people are. To provide some sort of encouragement and comfort, I wrote the words "YOU CAN DO IT!" on a little piece of paper and put it in my shoe every time I gave a talk. I knew that those words would be supporting me throughout my speeches that I would be standing on a message of success. Whenever I got nervous, just thinking about that message "under foot" made me smile. I was standing on top of that belief.

• Hold Cheerleading Tryouts

Why not try out Inner Cheerleading and see for yourself? Create a few cheers that align with your current goals and see how they work for you. Practice one or two important cheers every morning for a month and watch how things change. Keep track in a notebook. Write your cheers and also the results that come because of doing them.

When we held cheerleading tryouts, we had a checklist of things we looked for in a cheerleader: her smile, her ability to design a great cheer, her performance level, her confidence level. Write a list of the things you want that new cheer to do for you. Measure it. Track it. And correct as necessary. If someone did not make the cheerleading squad after trying out, they could always try out again after learning what they needed to improve.

In the same way you must ask yourself what is not working and then correct it in order to get it right the next time.

• A Knock-'em-Over Strategy

When a fearful thought pops up in front of me, I find it effective to take the offensive - not to shrink in fright or become paralyzed. Charge right through that thought as a linebacker does. Knock it down and keep moving. Your emotional state should immediately feel better.

> Fear thought: *You can't do that!*
> Knock-'em-over thought: ***Says who?!***

The idea to gently turn away from rising negative thoughts while meditating may work for others, but it did not always work for me - so when I would get anxious as these thoughts came up, this technique cleared the menacing emotions and thoughts away. See those thoughts and just drive right over them. Do not worry. They will not get up and follow you.

• Get Into The "Vacation" Feeling

When you take a vacation, you just can't wait to get up and get going. Start your day that way - fresh, anxious to begin the wonderful new day life has in store for you. Cheers can do that for you.

Do 3-5 cheers each morning to wake up your motivational muscles, muscles that help you take effective actions toward your goals. Think of the most pleasant vacation you've ever had. Put that feeling into your words as you cheer for yourself. Watch a magical day unfold for you. Cheers help you start your day with that "vacation" feeling. Why is any day different than a vacation? Because you *think* it is.

Make each day a vacation. Make each moment a vacation and you have found a secret to enjoying life.

• Sometimes Opposites Attract

If you're not happy with something, the opposite of your displeasure will often give you relief. So take it. Give yourself, and if appropriate, others, the opposite remark of what you are tempted to say. Look for the laudable qualities. If your roommate is messy or critical, look where they are organized or where they *do* give compliments. The good traits will appear when you put your focus there. Maybe it is just that you are not seeing them.

While I was at a life-changing seminar, a woman was having very negative feelings toward a particular man. The leader decided to investigate this and had them face each other. The woman was to tell her feelings to the man, while he was to send thoughts of love to her, which he did. We could all feel it.

She continued to accuse him of all sorts of things, until the facilitator finally asked her, "Who is he? Who does he remind you of?" She finally burst out crying, "My brother." The spell was broken.

Her brother had abused her when she was growing up. The eyes of this man reminded her of that brother - even though this new man was a beautiful soul who only felt protective and caring toward her. She had colored all men with the eyes and behavior of her brother. At last she could see with the eyes of truth.

• General Cheers are Generally Great

Generalized cheers are OK for half time, before the game and time-outs. Specialized cheers are for DURING the game when a specific result is desired. It's the same with your life when you cheer for yourself. When a specific result is desired in your life, like before you make an important phone call, do a specialized cheer such as: "I'd really like to be able to work with Kathy on this project," or ""To go to Houston would be so incredible. I would love it!"

But when you get up in the morning, do a bunch of general cheers. "I am great. I can win." This will get you in a generally good frame of mind and that will set up the day for your specific successes.

- **Cheer at The End of Each Day to Celebrate Your Achievements**

By acknowledging the small successes you have each day, you open the door for much larger successes to come in. It's a beautiful way to be thankful for the gifts each day brings.

"Great job! You finished that project, even though you were tired."

"Way to go! You cleaned the garage!"

"I'm so proud of you for honoring your word today, when it would've been so easy to quit."

Trust me, you'll be smiling when you finish.

- **The Magical Cheering Moment**

There is a special moment that can change your results, and significantly impact the outcome of what you are about to do.

Here's the secret:

Take a moment BEFORE you do something that is important to your goals, and do a cheer. Those 30 seconds or so will put you in the "goal" frame, the "touchdown mode," where you reach up and touch your dreams. Then take the action to deliver it. It is magical. It gives you a much better chance for success. Feel the dream before the action. Feel it completely. Even feel any fears you have. I recommend the wonderful book, "The Sedona Method", to teach you how to "feel" feelings.

I had a film script I wanted to send to a large company that could make it a success. The thought I used for that magic moment before the call was "This is the film they have been waiting for!" I really believed it too! They called back and requested to see the script.

On most phone calls, it will only take 30 seconds for your request to be granted – or not. Take an equal amount of time to get in a positive frame of mind. Then you will be "up" when you call, yet your voice will return to a calmer pitch that is much more favorable to getting what you desire. All that hidden, unexpressed nervousness and excitement comes out during your "cheers," and you will have a more natural, relaxed and pleasant feel to your voice - which the person on the other end of the phone will notice. If you don't have the motivation, chances are you won't take action. So encourage. Then act.

The MAGIC MOMENT of cheering for yourself is like finding a bottle with a genie in it. You must ASK the genie for what you want. I believe that if what you want is for your highest good and that of others, you WILL get it. That wish will be delivered. In the movie *The Princess Bride*, the hero says to whatever request his true love gives him, "As you wish!" - even if the princess didn't really *need* anything but was *testing* him.

This is a loving universe. When you get in touch with your true self and ask for your true desires, how can a loving universe, a loving God, not fulfill them?

Ask for and cheer for your goal before you take an action, rather than complain about it and feel bad after. Before is when you have the chance to alter the future and actually help predict your success in that action.

A coach takes the time before a game or a big play to really pump up the team or a specific player. That way they are READY to score. They KNOW they can score. They go out onto that field very motivated, not unsure, but bursting with confidence. You can do this too.

Those 30 seconds before you take an action to reach your dreams is affirming to God and the whole world that this is what you really want. Get clear about it and feel that clarity through your cheers in those 30 seconds.

This MAGIC MOMENT is the moment that makes your dreams come alive.

The Lesson: Include the MAGIC MOMENT
in every goal-oriented action.

But remember the goal of the cheers here: to transform your inner game so you will perform the actions to get you where you want to be in the game. The game of life is won first in the mind. It is an inner game and you need an inner tool. You are both the cheerleader and the player in your life. You are the leader! Be that hero.

Provide that inner leadership to yourself.

From watching the game, cheerleaders understand some deeper aspects of winning. What do cheerleaders **"know"** that helps them win at the game of life?

Chapter 9

WHAT CHEERLEADERS KNOW

I have my dad to thank for opening my eyes to the fact that
when push comes to shove,
the shove that will get you across
the line in any form of endeavor, sport or life,
is the shove that must come from within you.
Jack Nicklaus

WHAT CHEERLEADERS KNOW

If you can master the following wisdom, winning will come easier to you.

1.   CHEERS ARE FREE

Cheers do not cost anything. Best of all you can make them up on the spot, to fit the occasion. There is an infinite supply. Using them only increases their value. What commodity does that?

ESPN considers competitive cheerleading to be a sport. Later another ESPN columnist said, "Cheerleading is nothing but cheap entertainment." And they were both right! It does not cost you one penny to say "Way to go!"

When you get a free gift for success, use it. If someone unconditionally gave you $100,000 to grow your business, would you turn it away? Cheers are free. And the right cheers at the right time can create lots of success and income for you.

CHEER SUCCESS IN
SO YOU CAN WIN

2.   CHEERLEADERS KNOW HOW POWERFUL THE VOICE IS...and they use their voices for success

Other people are affected by what you say, we agree:
and you can, if you want, by a kindly word
timely spoken, uplift somebody's life.
If this is true then surely you can uplift your own life,
since you are the recipient of the
cumulative effect of every word you speak.
Dr. Robert Anthony

A group of people with the same message can be very powerful. Individual cheerleaders merge with other cheerleaders to form a team that is bigger and stronger than she or he is alone. The squad can affect the crowd. The crowd sees in front of them a "positive energy" force.

Your voice, your breath, are powerful. Your spirit rides out on your breath. What are you sending out with your voice?

In *Even Cowgirls Get the Blues,* author Tom Robbins writes: "Sound travels through space long after its wave patterns have ceased to be detectable by the human ear." That means that people are affected by the vibrations of what you say even when they can no longer hear you! That is powerful!

Your Voice as an Individual is Powerful but As a Group You Can Command the World

The same words multiplied by 200 or 500 people give a stronger message to the fans and the team. If you can get 200 people to talk about your message, your team just may win.

The voice in a group can be used several ways. Each voice can join with another to make a powerful swell, to make a great sound. Or each voice can tell another voice and that voice tells 30 more. Before you know it, you have the next *Harry Potter*, the next bestseller, on your hands. That collective voice is strong.

Cheers for the President

I had a professor in college who once said to a class of about 25 people, "If everyone in this room would all support me and give me your time, talents and dedication, I could run for president and have a darn good chance of making it." He knew the power of people, of a dedicated cheering group. If those 25 people have a plan, and tell 25 others who tell 25 others, that is 15,625 people. If they take it two steps further, it is 9,765,625 people. Almost ten million people. That is only five levels of people. Not too bad! That is power. That is influence. That is how you become successful.

USE YOUR VOICE
IT'S A WINNING CHOICE

3. NEGATIVE CHEERS WORK AS WELL AS POSITIVE CHEERS, but cheerleaders don't use them

Keep away from people who try to belittle your ambitions.
Small people always do that, but the really great
make you feel that you, too, can become great.
Mark Twain

Just Following Orders

The first and great commandment is:
Don't let them scare you.
Elmer Davis

How many of you hear cheers that are bad for you or bad for the world? Whether these cheers come from yourself, from someone else or from the media, it is YOUR responsibility to only put or accept good cheers into your mind. Your mind will believe whatever cheers you put into it. It is a system that you command. It takes your orders, often literally.

The little ordering system master yells, "OK. Negative cheer coming through. Let's get on it and deliver!" And then you get what you don't really want!

But this ordering system also works to help you notice and confirm your good decisions.

Let's say you decide to travel to England. The subconscious then places your order to go to England. All around you, you'll notice signs of

England, trucks with the word "England" on them, castles in books, British flags, Bobbies and the like, to support that inner decision. England will seem to pop up everywhere. You change your mind and decide to go to Mexico. The order is placed to go to Mexico instead. You start to notice tamales and sombreros!

If you eat junk food and decide you want to get healthy, you have to stop choosing to eat it. If someone else feeds you junk food and you eat it, the result is the same - you do not get healthy. It does not matter *who* feeds you the negative input. It matters only if YOU eat it. You can refuse the junk food. It is your responsibility alone to do so. It is the same thing with negative cheers. You are the only one responsible for what goes into your brain and what stays there.

The More the Scarier

The problem with negative thoughts is that they always invite all their friends and family along. Let them in and they bring along all their relatives. They belong to a large unhappy family, an extended community of negative thinkers. And they want you to be as miserable as they are.

Would you invite termites into your home? Why would you invite negative thoughts or other people's words that will cause structural damage into your life via your belief system? That life-success belief system of yours is a most valuable asset. Treasure it.

Thinking About Thoughts

I reserve the right to disagree with myself.
Thom Rutledge

I have heard so many different statistics about thoughts. Some say we have this number of thoughts per day, some say that number. I have chosen an average of about 55,000 thoughts per day. Some people have more, some have less. But most of those thoughts are negative like, "I will look silly," or "I could get hurt." Statistics show that about 77% of the average person's thoughts are negative. Let's improve those odds.

Look how easy it is to change that percentage. If you have 55,000 thoughts daily with 77% of them negative, that is 42,350 negative thoughts every single day! Will your life go in a positive direction? I doubt it.

Think of those thoughts as money. Positive thoughts add money, negative thoughts subtract it. You put in $12,650 each day into a bank account but take out $42,350. You will become "positive thought bankrupt" in less than a day. Change the percentage and strengthen your positive thought muscles.

If you had just 51% positive thoughts, your life would be mostly positive. If you are average and increase your positive thoughts by 28%, then that 77 % goes down to 49% negative and 51% positive and you start winning! How do you do that? When you catch yourself thinking a negative thought, replace it with TWO positive ones. One to chase out the old, and the second to put a new one in its place.

Walking With Power

I usually take a walk for about an hour every day. OK, on busy weeks sometimes less. During that walk, I figured I think approximately 3,500 thoughts (55,000/16 [24 hours-8 for sleep]). So I have almost 4,000 chances to improve my life on that walk alone! I use that time to chant affirmations to myself. I use affirmations like, "I deserve success. Success comes to me easily and effortlessly. My decisions are good." I exercise my body and put my mind to work for my dreams. Sure, other thoughts creep in, but the vast majority of my thoughts during that walk are positive messages for success. I really believe this has worked some huge miracles in my life. And it can work in your life too.

Lighten Up Your Mind

Negative emotions and thoughts are like a dark coat of paint covering your brain. Your memory layers things as it stores them. Putting a positive thought and emotion in your mind (i.e., by thinking or remembering it) is like adding a thin layer of light paint over dark wet paint. It filters through and blends. It may take many layers of white paint to get to the point where the paint looks white instead of a mish-mosh of blended colors.

Get the color of life you desire through positive thoughts. Use plenty of them loaded with good strong emotions. Put a thought and a feeling together. It makes a "theeling." Right now, think about the happiest you've ever been. Now think, "I am rich." There may be some resistance to that thought or you would already be rich, but now some "white thought" paint will start to cover that dark resisting spot and will start blending through. Keep going with it. That is exactly what is supposed to happen.

Show Yourself the Money

I believe we get to choose our direction by choosing our own thoughts, our own cheers. Cheer for the direction you want your life to go. I was at a small seminar where a lady was protesting the advice of the leader, saying it was all fine and good but it just would not work for her. Sound familiar? The leader asked what her situation was. She said, "It's my job. When I go into work I feel like I lose my freedom." The leader asked if we could all help her think of something else to say to herself when she clocked in that would be more empowering. Before we could even give her any of our brilliant advice, she blurted out, "The money starts now!" What a great cheer! Clock in and think "Ca-ching!"

What if each thought were worth money to you? Do you think a thought like "Why does this always happen to me?" or "This shouldn't happen to me" will put money in your pocket? It may take out $100. A "Things shouldn't be so hard" thought may take out $500.

On the other hand, what if your thought is "I have an incredible future"? That thought may give you $1,000. Looking for a million dollar thought? How about "I am a millionaire and I create great value for the world with my life." If you truly believe it, feel it, know it, then it is a million-dollar thought. Use million-dollar thinking instead of "poor me" thoughts, and watch your odds improve in the game. Use positive cheers and your life will change. I am positive. Say it! Feel it and it is yours!

CHEER DON'T SNEER
STEER YOUR CHEERS

4. TO DO THE SPLITS, YOU'LL NEED TO STRETCH MORE

No, you do not have to do the splits to have an Inner Cheerleader, but are you curious how a cheerleader learned to do the splits? It takes perfection to do it right, and even a measly three inches from the floor will not look like the splits. Just as a cheerleader has to practice every day and stretch a little farther to attain her goal of reaching the floor, your Inner Cheerleader will have to do the virtual splits. When a cheerleader can do the splits, it looks effortless and it doesn't hurt at all. So too, will your virtual splits, whatever they may be.

In business, ask yourself, "What do I need to do a little of every day so I can accomplish my seemingly unattainable goal (my virtual splits)?" What can you do in your preseason business decisions that will lead you to achieve something that feels unattainable? Stretch yourself a little every day.

Make it just a little uncomfortable.

Then you will accomplish your goals.

GO FOR YOUR GOALS INCH BY INCH
PRETTY SOON IT IS A CINCH

5.   IT IS ABOUT THE GAME, NOT THE CHEERLEADER

The cheerleader knows she is a part of the game, that it takes many parts working together to make the game what it is. The cheerleader does not get caught up in her/his importance, but gets caught up in the game, the strategies, the fun, and the excitement of playing and not knowing the outcome. Sounds a lot like life.

When the focus is on the game, the strategies are usually apparent. When the focus is on the self, it is harder to know what to do, which makes it even harder to win.

When a cheerleader is out there cheering, she is too busy paying attention to the game to worry about her hair, the test next Tuesday, or what so-and-so said last week. The game takes the attention, and the cheerleader is part of all the fun, the drama and the outcome. Rather than diminishing his or her significance, this enlarges the life and role of the cheerleader. Funny, how looking outward at life and contributing to that game creates the exact thing you wish for, which cannot be created when you focus only on yourself. A cheerleader knows this.

Steven Covey has a great cheer:

DON'T IMPRESS...
BLESS

6.   WHEN YOU INCREASE THE TEAM'S SELF-ESTEEM YOU INCREASE YOUR OWN

Everything that you do or say that raises the
self-esteem of another raises your own as well.
Brian Tracy

Cheerleaders pass on self-esteem because they are doing something for someone else. They are lifting up the crowd. In lifting up others, you will be lifted up.

Years ago I taught aerobics at Rockwell International. A woman came up to me after working out. She was so shy, she had trouble saying the following words to me, "You know, before I started this class I could not make it around the track outside even once. Now I can do several laps!" She was delighted with this change. I was happy for her too. But I did not do the work for her. She did. I like to believe, though, that the class helped her get in shape so that her body cooperated with her desire.

Back then, my grandmommy Sally Ellen;
my granddaddy Ogden Judd;
and my dear aunts Pauline, Evelyn, Toddie,
Faith and Ramona would put me up on the
kitchen table at their farmhouse,
where I would dance and sing my heart out.
They'd whistle, cheer, and stomp their feet.
I see now how this really boosted my self-esteem.
Naomi Judd

THE HIGHER YOUR SELF-ESTEEM
THE BIGGER YOU CAN DREAM

7. GO FIRST

Be the first to cheer. Do not wait for someone else. You can encourage yourself and it in no way diminishes the message. If you encourage yourself first, you will notice that others follow your lead. But if you wait for others to encourage you, you might become dependent on them. Or needy. Or you might be waiting forever! You do not want to burden others with something like that. They will also respect you more if they can see that you are able to encourage yourself. Your encouragement is like a rod that forms in your spine, lifting you tall and strong, facing whatever the world gifts you with.

In the hugely successful play *The Producers,* Max Bialystock says to Leo Bloom in trying to convince Leo to go after his dream, "Yes, don't you realize, there's more to you than there is to you!" The line gets a lot of laughs because it's meant to encourage, yet further confuses the timid Bloom. Eventually Leo gets the message. Then he encourages *himself* to leave a very demeaning job.

Cheerleaders introduce themselves first. They perceive others as friends first. They smile first. That is how you get people to follow your lead. Leaders go first. Followers follow them. Cheerleaders know this.

The early bird still gets the worm.

The Lesson: Leaders must take the lead

GO FIRST

TO BE FIRST

8.   HAVE A MASCOT

They bring good luck. Have something fun and different like the Coca-Cola Polar Bear, Nipper, the RCA Dog, or the California Raisin. They are mascots for their companies. Many children have had their picture taken with Mickey Mouse. We are attracted to mascots. Like a logo that is recognizable or has a theme, mascots are cute and fun. They also do not talk. That is the cheerleader's job.

A white wing is my company logo. It's my symbol for a higher form of entertainment, beauty and joy. We are more likely to remember a company if they have a logo we can see and even more so if they have an identifiable mascot.

100 Miles of Cheers

The 100-Mile Endurance Run from Wrightwood to the Rose Bowl is a grueling footrace though the California mountains. In order to encourage the runners, who start at 5:00 a.m., the sponsors set up different checkpoint stations along the way. A middle-aged woman dressed in a colorful Hawaiian hula outfit greets runners at a midway checkpoint. Her job is to cheer them on. Another checkpoint has mascots dressed in gorilla outfits. These friendly, encouraging apes give the runners bottled water. There are also cheerleader support runners who run with the real runners to keep them motivated for a while. For most of their journey the runners are alone, so this effort really lifts their spirits and supports their souls and their goals.

We all need someone to run with us once in a while. These runners have a huge support team to ensure their 100-mile success. That journey of 100 miles up and down high mountain paths takes some runners less than a day, even though it is a day of very grueling physical and mental work.

One year, the final runner to actually finish the race and cross the line said, "I am the king. The first is the king and the last is the king." He believed he was a winner because he kept going to the finish and did not quit. Even though he could not possibly take first place, finishing the race was winning to him.

As an entrepreneur, your journey may be a one-year journey, a five-year journey, a ten-year journey or a lifelong journey. You will need some runners to help you. You will need some cheerleaders along the way. A mascot can be human, animal or symbolic. A mascot reminds you that the game is supposed to be fun. I have a little ceramic cheerleader statue that reminds me to encourage myself and to be cheery. Native Americans have a mascot in their dances in the form of someone who pokes fun at the seriousness of the dance. Have a mascot for balance. Choose something fun and motivating to be your mascot.

9. BE CONGRUENT

A cheerleader's body language, energy and words match. That is why people follow them. Because they trust them. Imagine a leader in front of a crowd saying, "We can do it! We will succeed!" A leader attracts and encourages people. A leader makes the crowd believe. A leader motivates. A leader leads. Everything about the leader shows that he or she is a leader. But what about someone who stands in front of a crowd, uncomfortable, unconfident, and unsure of him or herself? We do not follow those kinds of people. We are not attracted to leaders without charisma because we do not want to be like that. We want to be better than we are, and we want someone to show us how to do that. Everything about a cheerleader says "Cheerleader." You feel it. It's congruent.

In his Millionaire Mind Intensive seminars, T. Harv Eker says over and over: "How you do anything is how you do EVERYTHING." He uses this quote from Cheri Huber to illustrate that our beliefs affect us in every area of our lives. If we are miserly with others, we will be so with ourselves too. If we act generous to ourselves, we will be generous to others.

If You Have Conflicting Cheers...

Conflicting cheers are like pulling on a rope in two different directions. Where will you go? Probably nowhere if there is equal tension from both sides. If one side is stronger, that side will win, but it may not be the side you intended to win. Often these beliefs are unconscious. Then you get frustrated because you are "going nowhere."

Coach John Wooden mentored business executive and professional trainer Lynn Guerin. Guerin said, "Coach Wooden is the most consistent person I know." Wooden followed the same principles in his personal life as in the game.

Image is reputation. Character is who you really are. Get your image and your character to be the same. Being consistent in your life is like a beautifully decorated room. Everything works and goes together. An inconsistent life is like a messy room with decor that does not work or go together.

Get a theme. Choose a special theme for your life. Most people leave off the "e" and get a "them" life - a "parent's life," a "spouse's life," a "friend's life." Having a "life" theme does not mean you have a one-track life, but rather you have an overall consistency with your values and with who you are. For instance, let's take a movie, a romantic comedy. We pretty much know what to expect. But even in a romantic comedy there are some sad parts, some drama. Even in a high drama, we get some comic relief like Clint Eastwood's line, "Make my day." Have a "YOU CAN DO IT!" belief. It matches success.

MATCH YOUR BELIEFS AND ACTIONS
FOR LOTS OF GAME SATISFACTION

10. DO NOT USE PAPER POMPOMS

Early cheerleaders learned this the hard way. Pompoms were used in the 1930s and "officially" invented in 1956. After three decades of rain-soaked paper pompoms (cheerleaders are optimistic, right?), someone in the cheerleading realm finally figured out it would probably keep raining. They switched to vinyl pompoms. Do you have any paper pompoms in your life? Things that do not hold up in a storm? Get rid of them. Modernize.

Lean and Mean

I had the Leaning Gazebo of Yorba Linda, California. It was put up without a strong foundation, without any cement around the main posts. It fell over. It was rebuilt with just a little patch of cement around each post. A very heavy roof with lattice was stapled onto that. It leaned.

My daughter and I would pound nails into the sad structure to try to hold that gazebo together. It was a lot of useless work. One day a friend looked at it while he was helping me in the backyard. He got his hammer and started toward the gazebo with the intention of removing the leaning monster.

My first thoughts were "No, this is my symbol of an idyllic life, of harmony in the home. It cannot be destroyed." But I looked at the sad, leaning structure and decided to let it go. You know what? After that initial plunge into gazeboless land, I felt free. No more trying to hold together something that never was going to work. In place of the gazebo is a calm stone floor with an arbor, a soothing corner of rejuvenation. I threw out the paper pompom.

Pompom Bushes

The Bulgarians have a charming custom. On March 1st, their Marteniza Day, they send cards and flowers to all their friends to celebrate the end of winter and the beginning of spring. Attached to the cards are little red and white pompoms. They take the pompoms out to the garden and attach them to a bush. The colorful little pompoms cheer everyone up when they see them. They know spring is on its way.

There is actually a famous paper pompom. It is a book from the 16th century. The pompom book is supposed to contain the entire history of the world from creation to the 16th century, written on the separate strips of paper. Luckily no one took *that* pompom out into the rain.

11. EVERYONE IN THE CROWD IS IMPORTANT

How monotonous the sounds of the forest would be
if the music came only from the Top Ten birds.
Dan Bennett

Be like the sun. Shine on everyone.

I interviewed Adrea Muldoon, a fantastic dancer from Andrew Lloyd Webber's musical, *Cats*. She also worked in *Starlight Express* and toured with the Moscow Circus. Adrea said something I've always remembered:

"I learned it's important to give your all to every performance. Even when you're in a situation where you are the third girl in the back row, left hand corner, it's still important that you give your all because you are there for a reason. Maybe nobody can see you, or you think nobody can see you. Maybe nobody cares, but it matters. There's a reason you were put there, and you have to remember that. Sometimes it's tough. Sometimes it's hard to be in the back, working your can off and thinking nobody cares, but somebody does. And for me the highest honor I could ever achieve is the respect of my fellow performers, and you achieve that by giving your all."

You, too, are here for a reason, and there is an audience that needs you. Every player on a team or in a company makes a difference. Every person working in a supermarket or in an airport or in a school is part of a team that makes the whole thing work. Each needs to be respected for that position. Without them, it would not work. All honorable work is to be respected.

Ted Nicholas says, "I really do believe, and operate my life on, the premise that there are no unimportant people." Ted is a very warm person who absolutely reflected that attitude when I met him. Life rewards those who genuinely care about other people, like Ted does. Ted has sold more than 4 BILLION dollars of products.

Everyone in the crowd is important. Give them your best.

The Lesson: Sometimes the supportive role is the right one.
You don't always have to be the star.

FOR EVERYONE THERE
SHOW THAT YOU CARE

12. IF YOU HAVE A HUGE NEGATIVE EXTERNAL CHEERLEADER IN YOUR LIFE. OR WORSE, A WHOLE SQUAD, GET A HUMONGOUS INNER CHEERLEADER

...and for heaven's sake get rid of the negative ones.

"The efficient leader leads by encouraging, and not by trying to instill fear in the hearts of his followers."
Napoleon Hill

Fear can take you out of the game.

Do not surround yourself with "fear" leaders. A negative cheerleader is a "fear" leader. You will not achieve your goals with a fearleader on your team.

When you get pressure from all sides, you will either go up or down. Life always pushes you to become something bigger and better. When it does, your comfort zone no longer exists. You have to get a new comfort zone that embraces more. When you are feeling a lot of pressure, you can be assured you are being urged to grow.

There's an old saying that when you get squeezed whatever is in you will come out.
John C. Maxwell

LET GO OF THE FEAR LEADER

CREATE A CHEER LEADER

13. KNOW YOUR PURPOSE

Cheerleaders have a clear purpose. Their purpose is to encourage.

If it's in your blood you have to do it.
Frank Martin

Your life purpose is big. If you have little goals, which are very important to set, they are like a little practice football field. Your big goal, your dream, is like the Super Bowl, like a football stadium for the giants at Valhalla, the Nordic heaven.

But your life purpose is even bigger. Bigger than your dream. It is something that underlies everything you do, are and work toward. It is like being the color blue, or green. Once you know what "color" you are, you bring that color everywhere you go and "color" the scene with your unique life energy.

If your job here on this earth is to bring joy, you can choose to bring joy wherever you go. Let's say you choose to focus on a career that uses your talents in music. Your music will bring joy to yourself and to your listeners. But you can also choose to bring joy no matter where you are. You bring it to the supermarket, on the freeways, with your friends, at the bank, to the big, big football field of the world, because even beyond your goals, that joy is the essence of who you are.

Singer Donna Summer says every person has three main talents, but one of them needs to be put in front of the others. Know what YOUR "first" talent is. The talent that comes before all others. Donna's was music. When she put that first, everything flowed - because that is what she was meant to do. She was living her purpose. All your talents are valuable, but one needs to sit at the top of your success pyramid. Put your "first" talent there and the base of the pyramid will almost magically come into place. Once that happens, your other talents can play their supporting roles.

Purpose becomes a more powerful source of energy when it
moves from being externally to internally motivated.
Jim Loehr

Latent Gifts

Larry Phillips, the former Governor of the Pueblo of San Juan in New Mexico, showed me his gourd paintings. They were beautiful works of art, painted with ancient Native American symbols. Phillips said he himself was amazed because he did not even know this "art" was inside of him. Somewhere he had this ability stored away in his subconscious. And he was humbly in awe of his own gift.

What success, what talent, is latent in you, in that inner doorway of yours? When you find your talent, your gift, you will be absolutely astonished! When something amazes you that profoundly...it will also be amazing to the world.

Your Unique Life Formula

You were put here with a talent. You absolutely were. I have no doubt about it.

Remember high school chemistry? We each were given a unique formula in a test tube and had to decipher what the basic elements were. We had to conduct a lot of experiments and know what each chemical did when mixed with others. By the process of elimination, we came to discover what our unique blend was. Your talent and life purpose are like those chemicals. You probably don't know right away, what it is. A few lucky kids got extremely easy mixes and could tell right away. But for most of us this was a very complicated experiment. So many unknowns and so many potential answers.

To use your dream you have to go through the fire. In chemistry class we put those chemicals through the fire. We burned the heck out of those chemicals. But the chemicals, the core chemicals, stayed the same, like your dream. No one gets a dream without the fire to test it. Without the dragon.

Some people live their lives at the task level,
some people live their lives at the goal level,
but the happiest people are those
who live their lives at the purpose level.
Nido Qubein

The Lesson: Fulfill your role and you will create beautiful things.

14. EVERY ONCE IN A WHILE YOU HAVE TO LEAVE THE GROUND

Sometimes a cheerleader has so much joy inside, so much excitement and passion, that she jumps. She is jumping for joy. Every once in a while you get to defy gravity when you reach one of your goals. In leaving the ground, you are reaching your dreams. Do not be afraid to jump toward those dreams. There are lots of different kinds of jumps that cheerleaders do, but the important thing is that they jump with emotion and with success. You can too!

Show Your Stuff

I went to a lecture by Tom Wolfe, author of *The Right Stuff*. He was very interesting to listen to, but all of a sudden he took off into a litany of words that completely floored me. He showed *his* stuff with the most astonishing grasp of language and the power of words I have ever heard. Through those words he stretched my world. He had a magnificent command of language. I am still awed to think of it.

Don't be afraid to show the world your best stuff. It's the part of the game we love.

15. THINK BIG

I realized for the first time that I had been thinking too small
and it was interfering with my ability to express myself.
Donna Summer

"Go, Fight, WIN!"
Not "Go, fight and take a step forward."

Cheerleaders cheer for the touchdown, the basket, the whole she-bang, for the 100%.

They know they won't win the whole game on any one play, but they *cheer* for the Big Win as if it could happen at any time.

Go Higher Than You Think You Can

In junior college, my professor told me to check out a private university to continue my education. I called and got the tuition rate. Gulp! When I told my professor about the exorbitant cost, he said, "No problem. Just call them back. See if you can get a scholarship." I did call them back and scheduled a meeting at the financial aid office. When I went in for the meeting, I loved the school and knew I would just love learning there. But I had a bottom line with both the financing I needed and the timeline of finishing my degree. The university met every single one of my requirements. I ended up going to that school; a university that I thought was way out of my league. It was not.

You make it your league.

Sometimes the things you want for yourself are not high enough. Reach for the top shelf. It is where the goodies are stored. Out of sight of most people.

All the big moments of my life have been when I've reached higher and not settled, when I've raised my thinking, when I've used High Thinking.

Thomas Edison was not afraid to go big, and he was willing to pay the price to keep on going. He *knew* he could succeed. You probably won't have to do something 10,000 times like he did to succeed. If it is your vision, it CAN happen - if you decide it will. Think BIG.

> THINK BIG, THINK GRAND
> GIVE SUCCESS THE UPPER HAND

16.   CHEERLEADERS KNOW THEY ARE STRONGER TOGETHER

> *When you add others you add strength*
> Coach John R. Wooden

> *The environment that creates winners*
> *is almost always made up of winners.*
> Barbara Sher

As Shakespeare might have said if he was a sportswriter, "All the world's a game." And we are on the same team. Let's win this game together.

When legendary coach Vince Lombardi was asked the reason for his championship teams, Lombardi said, yes, they had great players, but it wasn't that. Yes, they had a great coaching staff, but it wasn't that either. Lombardi felt it was because the players truly cared for one another. They really loved everybody on the team and wanted everyone to win. When you join with people, you want them to win the game too.

All teams need those coaches and players, but they need cheerleaders too. They need someone to encourage the team and the crowd. They need to know someone cares. That is what a cheerleader does. Can you imagine a game without cheerleaders? Without the enthusiasm, the cheers, the pom-poms, megaphones and stunts?

Cheerleaders add the crowd's energy to their own to create a sea of enthusiasm, full of a winning attitude. Find the voices that will blend with yours to create success. Find those people saying the same things you do and team up with them. Joint ventures often create enormous success for those involved. Find strength in others, and your success will come faster.

FIND STRENGTH WITH OTHERS
WITH YOUR SISTERS AND BROTHERS

17. IF YOU'RE GOING TO GET THROWN…TRUST YOUR BASE

The base, the bottom of the pyramid or stunt, is voted the most diffi-cult position in cheerleading, with the flyer - the one who gets thrown - coming in second.

Your base is your gut.
Your flyer is your heart.

TRUST YOUR GUT
AND FLY WITH YOUR HEART

If you are truly flying with your heart,
you are ready for **bigger things in life.** Let's go!

Chapter 10

VARSITY

(When you are ready for the BIG game)

If we want things to change for the better,
we have to be the miracle.
Edward James Allen IV

www.yourinnercheerleader.com

WHEN DO YOU MOVE UP TO VARSITY CHEERLEADING?

Fear is bold but insists that you be timid.
Thom Rutledge

Y ou will be tested even more when you try out for Varsity cheerleading. These strategies are tougher because it IS tougher to make Varsity cheerleading. But you are also at the top so the rewards are even bigger. To get to Varsity you will have to face your biggest fears. All successful people have done that. Here's how.

You Go Through the Fire

I met Nina Saxon at a *Women in Film* meeting in Los Angeles. She is one of the top four title designers in Hollywood. You have all seen her work. Remember the opening scene from *Forrest Gump*? It was Nina who came up with the idea for the beautiful, floating white feather.

When Nina started her career in film she did not know anyone in Hollywood. Yes, she did go to USC, which helped. But her lucky break came when she got an interview with Michael Douglas to do titles for a movie called *Romancing the Stone*. Nina knew how important this interview was. And she was scared, very scared. She said she walked around the block at the studio about four times before she got up the courage to go in. But she did go in. And she did those titles and hundreds more after that. She went through the fire. You have to go through the fire to reach your dream. It's on the other side. The team, the Varsity cheerleaders, and the coach have been through the fire in order to play the game.

Do the "Unfear" Cheer

When you strive for greater things you will have fear. It is normal and natural. Varsity cheerleaders keep going through it.

EVEN THOUGH I AM AFRAID

I CALL UPON A GREATER AID

TO HELP ME THROUGH AND FIND A WAY

I TRUST THIS FEAR WILL GO AWAY

What To Do When a Cheerleader Needs Some Cheer

I had a really down day. A super-down day. So incredibly low that absolutely all the air went out of me, every ounce of energy. My home was for sale and I had accepted an offer. I was busy 14 hours a day packing to move a business and my home.

With only a little over ten days left to close escrow, I came back from a meeting late one night to find a phone message and fax. The fax said the seller was canceling escrow. It was completely unexpected.

All my energy for the upcoming move left in the instant I read that fax. I thought I could not go through all the effort of showing and selling the house again and was also pretty angry at the rude way the fax letter was written. That night I did not sleep very much.

The next day I had scheduled in my home a special Toastmaster's meeting in which I was supposed to give a speech. To top it off, the topic was supposed to be humorous, and *nothing* seemed funny right then.

Having no energy to have people over and certainly none to give a speech myself, I was thinking of giving the keys to my house to someone and just leaving. When I got past that thought, I decided I'd still have the meeting, but not give my speech. I would only listen to the other speeches.

But a persistent thought kept arising in my mind. My speech was about cheering people up. How could I give a speech about that topic when I could not even cheer myself up? Could this possibly be an opportunity to practice my own cheers? I got a new cheer.

WHEN YOU ARE SO LOW THAT YOU CAN'T CHEER FOR YOURSELF ANYMORE, REACH OUT TO SOMEONE WHO CAN.

And I gave that speech.

When you reach out, others do not have to reach as far to help you. Cheerleaders need to receive too. When your Inner Cheerleader needs to take the day off, let him. Nurture him and allow his friends to pick him back up.

Life is not about going it alone all the time.
It's about serving others and allowing them to serve you.
Karen Rauch Carter

People that day called me out of the blue to say "Hi." I told them what was going on and how I was feeling. One friend told me a story about timing. "Sometimes if a deal had gone through, you would not get what you really wanted. Trust that the timing is perfect," said my friend. Another emailed me to go outside and smell my beautiful flowers, then take a hot bubble bath with candles and music. Another sent me a psalm. One said, "Something even better will happen." All of these great and kind people, messengers of God, cheered up my Inner Cheerleader until she was strong enough to take a deep breath, pick herself up, dust herself off and start almost all over again.

David Ciambrone, the mystery writer, says that there is no such thing as writer's block. He believes it is just the universe putting up a big sign to go a different direction. If you are getting a big fat NO! in your life, use that valuable information. Change the NO to "know." Know that it is for a good reason and it will work in your best interests.

Being receptive to others who were cheering me was just as important at that point as cheering for myself. Because when I said, "You can do it!" every ounce of my being rebelled. I needed to feel these intense feelings fully and grieve a bit. Then I was ready to move on. Not before. My friends did what I could not. They put the cheerleader back in me.

You get no more points for going solo
than for getting a leg up.
Gail Evans

When you cannot cheer for yourself, when you are so low you cannot even say "Go, girl!" get someone else to cheer for you. Listen to affirmations. Use subliminal tapes. Call your friends.

When you are really, really down, allow others to cheer you UP.

Reach out. When you have fallen into the pits of life, if you can reach out even a little, someone else will be there to pull you up.

There ain't no cloud so thick that the
sun ain't shinin' on t'other side.
Rattlesnake, an 1870s' mountain man

Our energy is like a balloon. Sometimes it gets a little deflated by life. The Inner Cheerleader is like air that inflates our energy back up so we can fly again!

When you need a cheerleader and are feeling anything but enthusiastic, the Inner Cheerleader can bring those great feelings to you. You can call on your Inner Cheerleader whenever you need cheering up or encouragement. As your Inner Cheerleader develops and gets stronger, a large part of you will be more positive. As you use your Inner Cheerleader more and more, watch what happens in your life. It will be amazing.

The Lesson: A cheerleader goes to another
cheerleader when he is down.
He does not go to someone
who takes him further down.

MAKE THE BIG PLAY

Competitive greatness
is the enjoyment of a difficult challenge.
Don't be afraid to risk it all.
Coach John R. Wooden

Coach Wooden said that many players are afraid to take the "Big Shot" when it comes. If that "Big Shot" comes to you, will you take it? Wooden also said that competitive greatness is having the following belief:

I am my best when my best is needed.

When you are going for your goal, you will be given an opportunity to take a "big shot." Take it. To do so requires a lot of confidence in yourself. Know that that shot came to *you* for a reason.

Act on it.

When Your Big Play Comes

It is our duty as men and women to proceed
as though the limits of our abilities did not exist.
Pierre Teilhard De Chardin

My friend Standing Deer is the son of Medicine Mountain, the medicine man of Taos New Mexico. Standing Deer told me he was spending a lot of time in the Kiva with his father. I asked him what they were doing. "Working with energy," he told me. His father told him that when your energy comes, you have to be ready for it. In other words, there are some big moments, big waves of energy that cycle to us. We must be ready for them by "seeing" them. We must let that energy flow through us into the world. Otherwise we have to wait until the energy cycles again.

My Big Play

My Big Play came completely unexpectedly, as most Big Plays do. I had just bought a piano after being pianoless for a whole year. It was delivered late on June 7, 2004. That evening, I was so grateful to finally be able to play all the songs I had written. They felt like old friends. A new song started to come through and I pushed it away.

The next day that song insisted I listen. The song started out kind of sad and I really wondered why I would be writing a sad song when I was so very happy. As I continued to play the song, it got more uplifting. Finally, the words came and I realized that I was writing a song as a tribute to President Ronald Reagan's life. He had just died on the 5th. The feeling of having this happen was immense. Then the question was "What to do with it?" I made a great number of phone calls. One of them was to the Nixon Library because I had done a filming there with James Roosevelt. I figured they could get me through to someone at the Reagan Library.

The next day I got a call from the concert director of the Nixon Library. She asked about the song. I told her that I had just written it. I mentioned the special bond Reagan had with his wife, Nancy and how that was woven throughout the song. She asked if I would play the song that Sunday. They were having a tribute to Ronald Reagan. Before I could stop myself I said, "Yes."

I had just a few days to prepare and then perform the song. I had never performed in public before and I woke up in a complete panic thinking, "What have I done?!" But I worked through it and got to the point where I was going to do it no matter what because I wouldn't be able to live with myself if I didn't take this opportunity. The thing that got me to that feeling was that I knew it was a Big Play. The song had what I call Big Medicine - almost a life of its own. It came through me with a great number of miracles along the way. For instance, when I finished recording the song the first time, I looked down at the number of measures and thought, "Why am I looking at the measures?" It read "93." Then I thought, "What does that 93 mean? I wonder if that could possible be the number of years that President Reagan lived?" Sure enough, he lived for 93 years.

This was a Big Play. It came to me out of the blue. I had to see it and act on it. I had to face enormous fear in order to become as big as the song was. It was a gift not only to me, but to others. It was playing that song that pushed me through to a whole different level of life. And that is what a Big Play is all about.

RECAP

The goal of cheering: to effectively lead a crowd in support of an athletic team, and to generate spirit and pride within a school and community. It is one of the most important school leadership groups. Cheerleaders promote enthusiasm and positive attitudes.

Your goal: to win the game of life. The life that you want, desire and create. That's what makes you your own hero. Play fair. Set rules so it is a good game. When the game is done, OK. It is over. Over and Out.

Developing your Inner Cheerleader can create the following benefits in your life.

1. **Physical.** Cheers energize you to move. They "create" energy for you that you can use to accomplish your goals. The extra energy is what you want here, the positive and motivating energy from doing the cheers. Because of the physical movements of doing some cheers everyday, I lost those last 7-10 pounds when nothing else seemed to work. I include a twisting movement with the cheers. I initially used cheers to motivate myself, and found that it led to a trimmer waist and a loss of that unwanted weight. That was a surprise benefit. Movement is your big key to gaining more energy.

2. **Mental:** You gain more mental clarity when you think of the cheers that will lead you to the success you want. Your brain becomes focused like a laser. When I did this, my mind let go of anything that was not related to the result I wanted. This took some time but I found that it increased greatly at a certain point in the process. That is when I noticed it, and it continued to really accelerate the results in my life from that point on. This will happen to you as you do your own cheers.

3. **Emotional:** If you do your best, stay focused and do something toward your goals every day, your life will not be devoid of emotions, problems or challenges. But when they come, you'll be better able to handle them. And when things do go your way, you'll be better able to enjoy them.

4. **Spiritual:** When you start thinking of the game of life and everyone involved in the game, your focus changes and you want EVERYONE to win. We do not have physical games like that yet in sports, but maybe someday we will. Games where everyone does their best and both teams win. Perhaps the closest thing to this is the home show *Trading Spaces*, where both sides decorate the other's home, taking into consideration what each side wants and doing their best to give it to them. Once in a while a decorator will put her own ideas into the place, knowing that it was not the request of the homeowner, but usually both sides do win. An Inner Cheerleader will give you the encouragements that not only help you in your life but show you ways to help others make their lives better. This results in a much better world and better lives for those of us living in this world.

This is what I've learned from using the cheerleader in my life and doing cheers for the successes I desired. That Inner Cheerleader has taught me a lot. I would love for these cheering ideas to benefit you and help you achieve some of your cherished goals. Take these tools a step further and come up with your own cheers. Cheers that motivate YOU. It is your turn to win. It is your time.

Step into the circle of cheering.

You deserve that circle of success.

You deserve to fully enjoy the game of life.

www.yourinnercheerleader.com

Chapter 11

YOU TOO CAN DO IT!!!

Encourage one another.

Heb. 3:13

I say, the more we help each other,
the more we all move toward greater success.
Our real mantra should be "We can do it."
Gail Evans

With positive internal dialogue,
we can create self-power.
Deepak Chopra

www.yourinnercheerleader.com

Your Inner Cheerleader:

Confident, considerate, cooperative, determined, enthusiastic, honest and truthful, a leader, an optimist, responsible, and self-disciplined. Wouldn't you love to have this person on your side? You can.

The "cheer" leader is a fantastic part of you. (They're not called "cheerfollowers"!) The world would be a better place if we would stop trying to get things from others. Get things from within. Be the source, because within you is the source.

If you never got the encouragement you needed in your life - give it to yourself now! So what if it didn't happen in the past. Do it now! That's like saying "I never got to take a boat ride while I was growing up." The boat is here, my friend. Get in and enjoy the ride!

Inner CHEERLEADER or HECKLER? Which one are you and what is it doing to your life? Chose to spur your life on to victory and CREATE A FANTASTIC CHEERLEADER FOR YOURSELF.

By now you have become a fellow cheerleader. Thanks for taking this journey with me.

Remember that football field at the beginning of the book? Let me continue that scene...

My heart was absolutely overflowing as I thought, "God, help me to always remember this moment, this feeling."

It took me awhile, but I did remember... because you can't forget love.

You each have something that gives you that kind of feeling. Find it and express it, because that is your gift to the world. That is your cheer. That is how you become a hero.

CHEER YOURSELF ON

JUMP AND YELL

IF YOU DON'T YOU CAN NEVER TELL

WHAT YOU MIGHT BECOME, ACHIEVE AND DO

BY GIVING A VOICE
TO THE HERO IN YOU

You were all meant to be winners. You were all created to win at the game of life. So take it. Take your chance and give yourself the life you deserve. You can do it!

Aristotle said "... for the hardest victory is over self" and I believe that it is the only victory, the one that truly matters in life.

Cheer for yourself even when it feels the most difficult. That is when the rewards in life cannot wait to get to you. That is where success lives.

You have already won a spot in the game of life.

Play it well.

Abundant cheers to you,

Terri Marie

Appendix

Find or create the voice within that says,
"You can do it!"
Joe Vitale

Appendix A

AFFIRMATIVE ACTION

The truth is that the greatest opportunity
you have, is to change who you are.
John C. Maxwell

Cheers are affirmations with a twist. This tool will help make you more successful and reach your goals.

Affirmations are like food. You use them up. You burn them off. So you constantly have to feed yourself more of them.

Although I do believe affirmations work, I think it's about saying the best affirmation for *you*. When you install your perfect new internal programming, you can achieve your unique life purpose.

If your purpose is to be a speaker, then a good affirmation could be, "I am poised and communicate clearly." If your purpose is to be a writer, you might just want to say, "I communicate very clearly with deep insight." A doctor could cheer, "I am a caring, loving person."

How will you know if you have done enough affirmations?

Because of the results in your life. Money WILL be easy to get. You WILL have what you want. You WILL have clear insights. You WILL be loving or whatever it is that you have cheered for.

Emfirmations

An affirmation by itself will definitely do some good for you, but if you add emotion – I call it an "emfirmation" - it is more than twice as powerful. And if you add a physical movement to the other two, you add a strikingly good chance of achieving your desired result. A cheer does this. It is an affirmation that rhymes – the most powerful kind. It has emotion – happily yelling your cheers! And it includes doing physical movements – the cheer routines.

We all have different emotional scales. Think of emotions as pounds. If you step on the emotional scale of anger, it may read 250. If you step on the emotional scale of joy, it may read 400. This can be represented by a bar chart. Every person's emotional chart is different. This chart changes every second, like a musical pattern or sound bar on a stereo. Life matches us to equal emotional partners. It has to balance this equation.

If your emotional scale of fear equals 150, you will attract those who also have an emotional fear scale of 150. If your emotional scale of patience equals 35, so will those you attract. And boy are you two going to have a challenge together! But that's how it works. Sometimes you are being matched with someone very angry when you think you are very kind and compassionate. That's because your shadow belief is hidden and you're not seeing it. You cover your emotion of anger with kindness and pretend the anger does not exist. That person, through their emotion, is showing you where you can look in the mirror and make a breakthrough that will give you much more happiness in your life. Yes, you can move on past this angry person, once you learn the lesson. Otherwise you get more angry people in different bodies. It is like repeating the same grade in school. Just learn the darn lesson and get it over with.

So when you are in need of a shot of something positive, use a cheer, an *emfirmation*. Feed yourself many of these during the day. They will not add weight to your body, but they will add a HUGE amount of weight to your goals.

Appendix B

POSITIVE CHEERS

*Gather enough people with positive energy... and you
can solve problems that would seem insurmountable.*
Ed Keller

Keep your cheers positive. Ask yourself if your current thoughts and cheers will create the great life you want. Positive cheers make you sparkle inside. Negative cheers bring a form of discomfort.

When you are playing your game, which of the following do you do?

Tackle a problem: Do not let your problems run all over your field. Go after each obstacle and remove it. The quicker you tackle them, the less damage they do. Become a bigger force than your problems and they cease to be problems.

Defend your receivers: Keep your receivers ready. Make sure you are always ready to receive the action that the Universe will throw at you. Make certain nothing is blocking your ability to receive.

Retrain: Teach your brain how to go after the goals you choose instead of letting whatever got in there run the show and make the plays.

One day on my walk, there was a little girl inside her house. I could hear her singing and clapping her hands. Her mother was playing with her. How wonderful the memories those two were creating! How great the programming! When we reprogram ourselves, we need to do things that bring that little child back into "play," because often that is where the "hurt" against success happened.

So if you have been trying to succeed at business and it's not been working, you may not have learned that it was safe to succeed, or easy to succeed, or that you are worthy of success. So you have to retrain yourself. Otherwise, when you go to make an important call or go to an important meeting, (which are two strong ways to succeed), your younger version of you throws a tantrum. It may not be as dramatic as stomping and crying. It may be getting another cup of coffee, turning on a TV program, getting tired, or deciding you have to clean up a mess in another area.

These are all ways that little tantrum thrower gets to avoid the success it fears. You must train her to be comfortable with success - to want it and enjoy it. Take her by the hand and say, "Let's have fun today. How can we make this business fun? How can we make calling this person fun?" If someone always said no when you asked for things, MOST LIKELY you will carry this over into your professional life, which does not serve you well. Retrain it. Be like that little girl, sing and clap. Program in the good stuff. The bad stuff will leave.

When you do the cheers you are having fun. You are retraining, working the success muscles. The cheers may seem like simple things but they are potent. Einstein created the most famous theory in history because of play and imagination. He had to allow himself the time and space to daydream that he was riding a sunbeam out into the universe.

Now can you imagine your boss comes in and asks what you are doing and you say, "I'm riding out on a sunbeam." You might not want to let the door hit you on your way out. We don't value this kind of thinking in our culture. But we need to. We need big dreamers to solve the big problems our world is facing. We CAN solve them. Creativity will be the tool, not doing things the way they have always been done, but in new, bold and brilliant ways. Ways of clapping hands and singing for the joy of life and living every moment fully. That is our destiny.

NEGATIVE CHEERS

A single negative thought is what gets you hit in the face.
Jim Mancini, middleweight boxer

Do you...

Run into difficulties?
Go out of bounds?
Jump to conclusions?

It can be easy to jump to the wrong conclusion. But it is a form of negative thinking.

$10,000 $10,000 $7,500

I had three offers on my house. The first person gave me a deposit of $10,000. The second, a deposit of $10,000. The third one cancelled the sale and we gave her back $7,500. Assuming that the buyer also gave me a $10,000 deposit, I asked my agent what happened to the other $2,500. It turned out the buyer had given me $7,500. I had jumped to the wrong conclusion.

Soften the Borders

There was a movie about a wife hidden in a suitcase by her husband trying to cross the border of the Iron Curtain. Many times the husband had carried a suitcase of books across the border. The suitcase weighed about the same amount as his wife did. The government officials checked the suitcase time after time and always found it filled with books. The husband finally tried smuggling his wife across the border inside the suitcase. The guards, expecting a load of books, waved them through. They got across the Iron

Curtain. This would have never worked the first time he crossed the border. But this time the guards jumped to the wrong conclusion, the one the husband hoped they would believe.

Ring Around the Conclusion

Years ago, after my divorce, I went into a pawnshop to sell my diamond ring because I needed some money. The guy looked at the ring, which was the engagement ring, not the wedding band. He rudely said, "I see you did not even make it to the altar." I had been married 16 years! A big jump to the wrong place!

In the above cases, conclusions, not goals were jumped to. Only in the above story about the Iron Curtain did the outcome have a positive effect because of the gamble the husband took. But the guards "lost" because they were the one jumping to the conclusion that the suitcase was filled with books again. When your mind has been trained to jump to a negative conclusion, you must retrain it to turn from that negative thought right before it "jumps." Catch it and have it "jump" in another direction - towards your new positive goal.

In the movie *Breakfast at Tiffany's*, a woman is looking in the mirror during the party scene, talking coyly to herself (with a drink in hand, I will add), laughing and being highly amused. Later at the party, we see the same woman sobbing in the mirror. What did she have to tell herself to go from a high state of enjoyment to the hysterical self-pitying woman in a matter of minutes? In the movie it is very funny, yet we do that too, by what we tell ourselves. We will not get upset if we do not tell ourselves bad or sad things. Tell yourself glad things. You can use the same ability the woman in the movie had in reverse and cheer yourself UP.

TO GET OUT OF FEELING SAD
REMIND YOURSELF OF FEELING GLAD

Are you spreading cheer or are you spreading fear?

The wrong cheer: "I can't do this."

The right cheer: "I CAN do this."

Say it with spine straight. Chin up.

Stand up. Make yourself one-inch taller. Don't you feel more confident? Your energy rises. Every inch helps. It is not how tall you are. It is how much of your spirit fills you. It is how big your heart is.

Tipping the Balance

Once you have put enough positive input into your mind, your life will have to go in a positive direction - just as you keep turning a car in the direction you wish to head every time you start to go to a bad "area." If you keep from driving to where you've always gone, you can finally get the on the road you really want take. When the mind is full of positive, constructive thoughts, the life having those thoughts will have to be positive too. Then the score in your life changes and you will win. More positives than negatives!

www.yourinnercheerleader.com

Appendix C

FAMOUS CHEERLEADERS

Here are some of your fellow cheerleaders and what they have done with their lives. They are leaders who used their motivational skills to become very successful. Some have even led nations. The cheers may have helped the songwriters in this list create great rhythms and rhymes.

Franklin D. Roosevelt	U.S. President
Aaron Spelling	Filmmaker
George W. Bush	U.S. President
Paula Abdul	Songwriter
Ann-Margret	Actress
Halle Berry	Actress
Reba McEntire	Singer/actress
Sandra Bullock	Actress
Kim Basinger	Actress
Thad Cochran	U.S. Senator
Trent Lott	U.S. Senator
Phyllis George	Former Miss America, CBS Sportscaster
Susan Lucci	TV Actress
Jessica Lange	Actress
Jack Lemmon	Actor
Deana Carter	Singer
Katie Couric	Co-Anchor, Today Show
Madonna	Singer
Barbara Hershey	Actress
Jamie Lee Curtis	Actress
Sally Field	Actress
Michael Douglas	Actor

Calista Flockhart	Actress
Ruth Bader Ginsburg	Supreme Court Justice
Samuel L. Jackson	Actor
Diane Sawyer	Co- Anchor ABC News
Steve Martin	Actor
Mandy Moore	Actress
Shirley MacLaine	Actress
Sissy Spacek	Actress
Lily Tomlin	Actress
Vanna White	TV Personality
Cybill Shepherd	Actress
Teri Hatcher	Actress

And many, many more....

There is a serious side to cheerleaders. There is a lot more to cheering than most people know. There are millions of cheerleaders going through life applying these skills.

Perhaps YOU will be the next famous cheerleader!

Appendix D

CHEERING STRATEGIES LIST

THE CHEERING SECTION

1. Qualities of a Good Cheer
2. Potent Cheers
   - I CAN DO IT!
   - Do the Thirty-Second Cheer
   - Add a Physical Movement to Your Cheers
   - Use the Replay Effectively
   - Do the Opposite Cheer
   - It's Just a Game
3. When You Do Any Cheer:
   - Use High Energy
   - A Visual Image
   - The Release
4. Cheers for Different Occasions
   - Cheering Up Cheers
   - Cheers for Trust
   - Cheers for Motivation
   - Cheers to Go Through Fears
   - Favorite Cheers

VALUES

1. Believe You Can Win
2. Cheerleading is Addicting
3. Be Flexible
4. Cheerleaders Know They are Not the Team
5. Have Great Values

BEFORE THE GAME

1. Before The Game Practice Your Routines
2. Go to Training Camp Every Summer
3. Start Every Game With a Clean Slate
4. Make Signs to Encourage the Team
5. Have an Egg Sale
6. Come Up With New Routines
7. Never Get on a Bus Alone With the <u>Whole</u> Football Team
8. Remember Your School Song
9. Surround Yourself With Other Cheerleaders
10. Always Be Willing to Promote Your Team
11. Hold a Pep Rally

DURING THE GAME

1. Start The Game With a Big Kick-off
2. Give it as Much Energy as You've Got
3. Build Lots of Positive Energy
4. Stay in Synch with Your Team
5. Use Short Cheers When The Game is Moving Fast
6. Assume the Crowd is on Your Side
7. Know Your Game...and Know What Part of The Game You are In
8. Keep Going, Don't Drop the Ball
9. Celebrate Every Accomplishment
10. Read the Fans
11. Get the Message Across Quickly
12. Cheerleaders Don't Stand in Front of a Crowd and Think, They YELL
13. Keep Cheering Even When You're Not Ahead
14. Don't Turn Your Back on Your Fans
15. When Motivating Others, Encourage, Don't Force
16. Be a Cheerleader, Not a Firefighter

17. Repeat Yourself For Emphasis and Keep it Simple

18. Let Each Team Member be Viewed to Their Best Advantage.

19. Use Time-outs to Remotivate and Do Something Big

HALFTIME

1. Halftime is a Time to Regroup

2. Halftime is a Time to Show Your Best

3. If You Want to Wow the Crowd, Do a Flip

BACK TO THE GAME

1. When You Do a Stunt You Have to Commit 100 Percent

2. Be in the Moment

3. Every Second Counts

4. Spell Things Out for Extra Impact

5. Connect

6. Respect the Turf of Others

7. Don't Mind the Elements

8. *Love* Every Minute of The Game

9. Do Only One Cheer at a Time

10. Don't Make Excuses

11. When Cheering, Look Up - Not Down

12. Sometimes You Just Have to Float

13. If You Want to Attract Attention – Get Out in the Field

14. Smile

15. Cheer for the Team You Are Given

16. Cheerleaders Yell. Yell Loud

17. You are Always on Display, Every Word, Every Action

18. Share Responsibility

19. The Order In Which You Do Things is Important

20. Be Willing to Make the Call

21. It's Never Too Late to Win

22. Without Action You Do Not Win

23. Cheers Cleanse the Subconscious

AFTER THE GAME

1. There is Always Another Game Unless It's The Playoffs

2. After the Game Go Out For Pizza and Root Beer

WHAT YOU CAN LEARN FROM THE GAME

1. Be A Good Receiver

2. When You Fall Down, Get Up

3. The Huddle is a Still Point

4. Even When a Goal Seems Like the Long Way Home...Keep Going

5. There Rarely is a Straight and Narrow Path

6. Stay Out of the Way of the Ball

7. A Good Coach Will Call a Time-out at a Critical Point

8. Let Go of the Old Game, Embrace the New One

9. You Can't Cheer Everyone Up

10. Aim for Your Goal Post

11. Cheers in Action

- Send a Cheer- a gram.

- Hold Cheerleading Tryouts

- A Knock 'em-over Strategy

- Get Into the "Vacation" Feeling

- Sometimes Opposites Attract

- General Cheers are Generally Great

- Cheer at the End of Each Day to Celebrate Your Achievements

- The Magical Cheering Moment

WHAT CHEERLEADERS KNOW

1. Cheers are Free
2. Cheerleaders Know How Powerful The Voice is... and They Use Their Voices Together for Success
3. Negative Cheers Work as Well as Positive Cheers...But Cheerleaders Don't Use Them.
4. To Do the Splits, You'll Need to Stretch More
5. It is About The Game Not The Cheerleader
6. When You Increase the Team's Self-Esteem, You Increase Your Own Self-Esteem
7. Go First
8. Have a Mascot
9. Be Congruent
10. Do Not Use Paper Pompoms
11. Everyone in the Crowd is Important
12. If You Have a Huge Negative External Cheerleader in Your Life, or Worse, a Whole Squad, Get a HUMONGOUS INNER CHEERLEADER and Get Rid of the External Ones
13. Know Your Purpose
14. Every Once in Awhile You Have to Leave The Ground
15. Think Big!
16. Cheerleaders Know That They are Stronger Together
17. If You Are Going to Get Thrown...Trust Your Base

VARSITY

1. You Go Through the Fire
2. Do the "Unfear" Cheer
3. What to do When a Cheerleaders Needs Some Cheer
4. Make the Big Play
5. Recap

Remember...

YOU CAN DO IT!

I CAN DO IT!

WE CAN DO IT!

Do Your Own Cheers

Here they are! Your personalized cheers.
List your goals. Then cheer your way to success!

Your Goals:

Your Cheers:

www.yourinnercheerleader.com

Quick Order Form

Email orders: info@yourinnercheerleader.com

Postal Orders:
White Wing Entertainment
P.O. Box 3325
Sedona, AZ 86340

Please send me _____paperback copies of
"Your Inner Cheerleader"

Name:_____

Address:_____

City:_____State_____ZIP_____

Telephone:_____

Email:_____

I would like a gift copy sent to:

Name:_____

Address:_____

City:_____State_____ZIP_____

Paperback is $17.95
Shipping is $7.00
Shipping each additional book to same address is $5
Sales Tax: Please add 10.725% for Arizona residents. Sorry if you live in AZ ☺
Ebook purchase at www.yourinnercheerleader.com

Author Terri Marie is available for consulting and seminars
Email: info@yourinnercheerleader.com
Get a FREE inspirational message for 52 weeks. Sign up for your
 "Cheer of the Week" at www.yourinnercheerleader.com

ABOUT THE AUTHOR

Terri Marie is a former cheerleader who wants to encourage you to reach your full potential. She wrote this book to encourage you to encourage yourself the way she once had to learn how to do in order to make her life start working. Terri Marie wants to save you the trouble of all that "learning" the hard way and help you learn "The Cheerleaders Way." (It's a lot more fun!)

As a producer Terri Marie has made over thirty documentaries, some airing on PBS and ABC affiliates. For years she had a column called *Heroes Among Us* in the Orange County Register and an exercise program *called The Great Body Escape.*

Can you feel her cheering for you right now? Go you!

Praise for "Your Inner Cheerleader"

Within the pages of Terri Marie's "Cheerleader" book is a technique that can blast you into success. Hold on, get ready, you are about to change your whole game. See you in the winner's circle!
> – John Assaraf, from the movie "The Secret"

Your Inner Cheerleader is well written, clear and easy to understand. It will undoubtedly help harness a person's greatest (and little understood) power of the subconscious mind. Congratulations on a fine piece of work!
> - Ted Nicholas, 4 billion dollar man
> The Success Margin

This book is a jewel! I have enjoyed it, learned so much from it, and am recommending it to all of my friends and clients.
> - Dottie Walters, President/CEO
> Walters International Speakers Bureau

This incredible book reveals how to embrace life and bring together your own personal group of cheerleaders to help you succeed in love, business, learning, and everything you every wanted to achieve. It is not a book you can read just once. I keep it close by to give me daily inspirations.
> – Al Galasso, Book Dealers World

I love Terri Marie's book, her, and her message. It gives you the power to fulfill your dreams. It plugs you into the source of magic and miracles. You don't need to be around cheerleaders. You just need to be one. This book shows you how.
> Joe Vitale, Author, "The Attractor Factor"

Terri Marie had been a cheerleader for thousands in the stands but when she needed help in her life, she realized she needed to become her own cheerleader. The idea for this book started as the focus of a speech to a group of professional speakers in Orange County California. As her coach we talked about the audience, what they needed, and what she had to offer. Right from the start the audience, both men and women, loved her topic of The Inner Cheerleader. For all those who were not in the room that night, this is your chance to discover and awaken the Inner Cheerleader. Terri Marie has shown the way. All you have to do is Follow the *Cheer*leader.

> - Jack Nichols, Speaker, Coach

Most self-help books tell you how to live a successful life. This book shows you how to make your life a glorious adventure while achieving peace, joy and prosperity.

> - John Harricharan, Best-selling author

"Don't let the title fool you. Every great entrepreneur has created a great inner cheerleader. Step by step, this book gives you success strategies in a new, fun and effective way."

> - Tom Antion, Internet Marketing Training Center of Virginia
> www.IMTCVA.org

Terri Marie's book, *Your Inner Cheerleader,* is an unexpected and total delight. Her concepts of being your own cheerleader are remarkable and on target. You can't help but smile and get inspired as you read her book and learn what you can do for yourself to make strong, positive changes in your own life.

> - Louis B. Cady, M.D. Diplomat, American Board of Forensic
> Medicine, Founder, Cady Wellness Institute

CPSIA information can be obtained at www.ICGtesting.com
Printed in the USA
BVOW031708021211

277467BV00001B/86/P